MAINE STREET MIRACLE

Saving Yourself And America

Copyright © 2009
by
David E. Robinson

MAINE-PATRIOT.com
3 Linnell Circle
Brunswick, Maine 04011

maine-patriot.com

"When the student is ready, the teacher will appear."

Just as all the truths of God's reality are basically simple once we let ourselves discover them, so MAINE STREET MIRACLE reveals the beautiful but simple truth of how the individual in America today can restore freedom. This book is free from hate, hostility or revenge. The positive, loving nature of its answers give it its great power. Its course of action is educational, revealing, and fun!

Read it and try its recommendations. You'll like yourself more for doing so. And your children will love you for it!

"The Matrix is a system, Newo, and that system is our enemy. When you are inside, you look around, and what do you see? You see businessmen, teachers, lawyers, carpenters; the very minds of the people we are trying to save. Until we do, these people are part of that system and that makes them our enemies. You have to understand, most of these people are not ready to be unplugged, and many are so hopelessly dependent on the system, they'll fight to protect it. The Matrix is everywhere. It is all around us. Even now, in this very room. You can see it when you look our your window, or when you turn on your television set. You can feel it when you go to work, when you go to church, when you pay your taxes. Its is the "world" that has been pulled over your eyes to blind you from the truth."

— Morpheus, in the Movie "The Matrix."

MAINE STREET MIRACLE

Maine Street Miracle

Contents

Appendix

MAINE STREET MIRACLE

Foreword

DISTINGUISHED economic experts, Nobel prize winners, and White House advisors notwithstanding, *Maine Street Miracle* contains *the only lawful and workable solution there can ever be to our worsening financial woes, public and private.* Amazingly, this solution is already with us, built into the mechanics of our government. But the design is such that the solution must be activated from OUTSIDE the government — by you and me — the people. The reason the solution has lain dormant for so long is that the people have *somehow* been kept unaware of the presence of the solution. Until now!

This book goes right to the Supreme Law of the Land to reveal that solution to us. Then, it shows step by step how the solution can be *achieved.* As each individual uses the United States Constitution to preserve the value of his own fortune, our decaying federal economic, political, and social conditions will begin to heal themselves literally overnight. This truly is the stuff of which miracles are made.

— *The Patriot*

"*From 80-90% of the population can be hypnotized in varying degrees. At least 5% (10,000,000) of the U.S. population is extraordinarily hypnotizable, so easily hypnotized that they are in a constant state of exaggerated suggestibility even when awake and going about their normal daily routine. They are at the TOTAL MERCY of all forms of influences and can easily be persuaded to do things, and afterwards have no idea why they did what they did. They go in and out of a trance-like state without even knowing what is happening to them. As a result, they suffer all kinds of problems without realizing the real cause.*"

"*The destruction of a mighty nation may well be approaching because of the activities of one person. He has encouraged leaders to tranquilize the populace with half-truths. He has lured the press into inattention and has assisted the people in duping themselves. He has persuaded his fellow citizens to concentrate on life's comic strips and mindless entertainments and to avoid the bruises of reality. . . . The culprit is the person whose eyes scan these words, and whose hands — at this moment — hold this book.*"

Come Out From The Idea-sphere

WE put a lot of faith in ideas. So much so that we're moved by them. We are tuned to the idea-sphere. We think life consists of choosing the best idea from the selection offered us; then living by our choice. We forget that the idea-sphere exists only in the mind. The mind is but a part of the whole individual, meaning that living only by ideas deprives the rest of oneself of many pleasures we were born capable of experiencing. Recently, a news story appeared in the world press about 14 Chinese children who could read with their skin. They could tell color when blindfolded, by touch. Doctors were amazed and puzzled. And then there's all the documentation of ESP, clairvoyance, telekinesis, and so on. The scientists who have sunk their lives into studying them maintain these phenomena are not weird but quite natural — ordinary abilities we are all born with in order to fully sense this world and live comfortably in it as participating organisms.

But beginning in our earliest years and continuing throughout our lives, these ordinary abilities are pushed into disuse by swarms of ideas — ideas that we are somehow "bad"; or "good"; or "Mouseketeers"; or "cereal lovers"; or "kids"; or "mentally ill"; or "Democrats"; or Republicans"; or "Senior Citizens." Where do these ideas come from? From those who profit by people's not using their natural abilities, where else? From those who stake claims of authority over helpless people. From those who are in the *business* of guiding and governing others. It's easy to see that if you can hook someone on an idea, on a dream, you can fleece his pockets. Reality overrules an idea every time. To keep control over people, you must keep the idea-sphere charged with images, hopes, suggestions, debates and alternatives, the same way radio and TV fills the atmosphere with pictures and sound. While the victim is lost in his dream, you can march stealthily into his stores and take what you want. With ideas, you can make him happy or afraid, dance or crawl, or prefer one product over another. You can make him kill, or build bombs.

But for all that ideas can make us do, they are only ideas. Dreams. I spent two terrified years in grammar school fearing graduation to Junior High School because of the hazing I would undergo. The idea-sphere resounded with reports of 7th graders getting heads shaved, and faces painted with red lipstick stripes, of being forced to push B-B's down the hall with their noses, of having to eat rotten eggs, or of having to walk home naked from some lonely spot in the woods. I suffered countless nightmares in apprehension of the coming of 'My Day.' But when my day came, nobody did anything to me. I went through hazing without so much as a lovetap from an upperclassman. After hazing week was over, I felt almost unwanted.

What happened? I know now that I had *withdrawn* from the idea-sphere at hazing time. When a hazer would come near me, there would be no transmission of look or feeling between us. No connection. Since hazing was but an idea, he could only pick up from *subscribers* to the idea. Believers. He could attack only those whose eyes said "Please don't haze me." Eyes that asked "What's hazing?" were ignored. They were no part of the idea-sphere. They were of another frequency completely. Of another world. This was one of my earliest lessons in the utter fraudulence of ideas and has often been the manner in which I have approached problems.

This little book is not about ideas, except to encourage you to shed them. I hope it will wean you away from the idea-sphere. This book is about a genuine, real thing you can touch. The difference between an idea and a thing you can touch was illustrated tragically to me years ago when a friend of mine, on LSD, thought he was pulling the trigger of a water pistol aimed at his temple but it was a loaded Colt .45! Ideas have their validity, but they're no match for reality. Reality overrules them every time. That's why, these days, I find it so hard to appreciate fiction. So much of what passes for reality today is fiction enough! The reality of this book is:

IF YOU DON'T LIKE WHAT'S HAPPENING IN YOUR LIFE, YOU CAN FIX IT.

You can fix it without cheating anyone; without counselling with experts; without subscribing to any newsletter that keeps you posted on inside info; without writing Washington or getting involved in politics; without organizing; and without spending a penny unless you choose to.

And a miracle will happen: as you fix what's wrong in your OWN life, you'll automatically be fixing what's wrong with America's well-being. Instantly you'll begin claiming your little-known and completely legal economic rights, good for hundreds even thousands of extra dollars in your family treasury, and not applying to government for it, either! Couldn't you use some extra cash in these raw times? The law provides benefits for you, regardless of your age, condition, financial status, sex, or whatever. Benefits to help you survive the ups and downs and starts and jolts of this fluctuating economy. But if you continue floating about in the weightlessness of ideas you'll never know how to claim these benefits. No. To experience THIS miracle, you must be down to earth.

I've shown this manuscript to people who can be counted on for merciless feedback. Any one of them could have halted this publication simply by responding with faint praise. But the unanimous verdict seems to be "At last, a book that describes the problem and then gives a DIRECT, QUICK, NATURAL SOLUTION." I believe in direct quick, natural solutions. I believe that when you have a mosquito bite, you should scratch it, not take Milk of Magnesia. Trying to solve one's own personal financial dilemma by appealing to the idea-sphere — government, federations, organizations, advisors, financial planners, experts — is submitting to surgery for that mosquito bite, a sad, tragic, waste of time, resources, and happiness.

I hope judges and mayors and court clerks, and all levels of government employees will read this little book, because it was written as much for them as for people in the private sector. I hope bankers and reporters and small businessmen and schoolteachers will read it. And attorneys, who call themselves our guardians of the law. And church folks should read it, too, because after all God is the foundation of all miracles, including the restoration of a happy America. I cannot describe how vividly my understanding of God progressed in me, from an idea to a touchable reality, as this book developed. Perhaps you will sense it as you read on.

Dream worlds are hard to leave. Even *painful dream worlds* are hard to leave. They're especially hard to leave when the dream makers tell us that leaving the dream world will be catastrophic. Many people actually *prefer* the idea-sphere to reality, not caring that they are denying their whole selves pleasures of incredible intensity, pleasures and abilities truly "undreamed of." These people, and they are among our most respected citizens, are fully trained to believe in the life being broadcast in the idea-sphere, and they believe it can't get much better than it is. They'll never come around to reality until they are forced to.

This little book can only switch on the lights for people who are already tossing and turning under a terrifying yet fascinating nightmare. Suddenly, you bolt awake and there are your walls, the pictures, the lamps, the quilt, the soft breathing of your family. What had been twisting your body and mind was nothing but ideas, and they scamper away as soon as you open your eyes to the glowing warmth of the real world.

We don't need to *restore* the American Dream; we need to *wake up from it.*

"*Thou shalt not have in thy bag divers weights, a great and a small. Thou shalt not have in thine house divers measures, a great and a small. But thou shalt have a perfect and just weight, a perfect and just measure shalt thou have: that thy days may be lengthened in the land which the Lord thy God giveth thee.*"
—*Deuteronomy 25:13-15.*

"*The world has always been betrayed not by scoundrels but by decent men with bad ideas.*"

"*By a continuing process of inflation, government can confiscate, secretly and unobserved, an important part of the wealth of their citizens. There is no subtler, no surer means of overturning the existing basis of society than to debauch the currency. The process engages all the hidden forces of economic law on the side of destruction, and does it in a manner which not one man in a million is able to diagnose.*"

1
The Gathering Storm

"BLOOD running in the streets. Mobs of rioters and demonstrators threatening banks and legislature. Looting of shops and homes. Credit ruined. Strikes and unemployment. Trade and distribution paralyzed. Shortages of food. Bankruptcies everywhere. Court dockets overloaded. Kidnappings for heavy ransom. Sexual perversion, drunkenness, rampant lawlessness" and so forth.

One distinguished politician writes to another: "The wheels of government are clogged, and we are descending into the vale of confusion and darkness. No day was ever more clouded than the present. We are fast verging to anarchy and confusion."

Where, when, and whom? Get ready for a shock: America, 1786 — ten years after the signing of the Declaration of Independence. The correspondence was from George Washington to James Madison.

On February 3, of the following year (1787), Washington wrote to Henry Knox: "If any person had told me that there would have been such formidable rebellion as exists, I would have thought him fit for a madhouse."

What went wrong? What forced this noble new country into conditions far worse than the tyranny against which it had declared its independence in the first place? The history books tell us it was a complicated variety of interrelated things, but the reality tells us it was only one: the money issued by the Continental Congress and the states' banking houses was paper that could not be redeemed for gold or silver coin. Inflation, *that* was the issue that had sunk George Washington to the depths of despair.

The paper currency of the Congress was printed in such exorbitant amounts in relation to the precious metals they represent, that wages and prices skyrocketed, forcing the Legislature to enact harsh wage and price controls. When these failed, moral-sounding laws reeking of piety and patriotism were enacted in an attempt to chain the people under penalty of violence to the government's absurd money:

> *If any person shall hereafter be so lost to all virtue and regard for his Country as to refuse to accept its notes, such person shall be deemed an enemy of the Country.*

This amounts to a law protecting bad-check artists, and so the people naturally ignored it and others like it. The depreciation of paper currency relative to coin followed the same sickening course our paper currency is following today.

DEPRECIATION OF CONTINENTAL CURRENCY AGAINST THE SPANISH MILLED DOLLAR, 1779.

January 14 . . . .
February 3 . . . .
April 2 . . . .
May 5 . . . .
June 4 . . . .
September 17 . . . .
October 14 . . . .
November 17 . . . .

In January, 1781, these notes were redeemable 100 to 1; in May, 1781, they ceased passing as currency and quietly died in the hands of their owners. Repeatedly, new series were issued, only to follow a similar pattern. A contemporary of the Revolution, Peletiah Webster, records it this way:

It ceased to pass as currency (in May, 1781), but was afterwards bought and sold as an article of speculation, at very uncertain and desultory prices, from 500 to one thousand to one.

Yet another contemporary writer, gives us this ridiculous aspect of inflation's ultimate achievement in the 1780's:

The annihilation was so complete that barber-shops were papered in jest with the bills; and the sailors, on returning from their cruises, being paid off in bundles of this worthless money, had suits of clothes made of it, and with characteristic lightheartedness turned their loss into a frolic by parading through the streets in decayed finery which in its better days had passed for thousands of dollars.

Again, Peletiah Webster writes:

Paper money polluted the equity of our laws, turned them into engines of oppression, corrupted the justice of our public administration, destroyed the fortunes of thousands who had confidence in it, enervated the trade, husbandry, and manufactures of our country, and went far to destroy the morality of our people.

Describing inflation to someone who has never experienced it is like describing the pain of fire to someone who has never been burned. You really have to live it to know how terrible it is. More than one Biblical scholar who has felt inflation concludes that the Beast in Revelation is nothing less than inflation itself. The worst thing about inflation is that there are so many *apparent causes* of it. The long-winded debate over *cause* only gives inflation time to spread and destroy more. The debate of cause is usually conducted by the many people who *benefit from inflation,* those who are first in line from the printing press, able to buy goods at current prices with money that soon raises the price of everything as it goes into circulation, increasing the volume of the money supply. It doesn't take much digging to know who the first-in-liners are: they're the beneficiaries of government programs, and of course the people, very few of whom are going to want to put their heart and soul into an effort to stop inflation. Why should they, when inflation is the secret of their success? They're not villains or conspirators. They're "Friends of Paper Money." There have always been "Friends of Paper Money" and they really cannot be blamed for doing anything evil or wrong.

What happened? I know now that I had *withdrawn* from the idea-sphere at hazing time. When a hazer would come near me, there would be no transmission of look or feeling between us. No connection. Because hazing was an idea, he could only pick up from *subscribers* to the idea. Believers. He could attack only those whose eyes said "Please don't haze me." Eyes that asked "What's hazing?" were ignored. They were not part of the idea-sphere. They were of another frequency completely. Another world.

This was one of my earliest lessons in the utter fraudulence of ideas and has often been the manner in which I have approached problems. This little book is not about ideas, except to encourage you to shed them. I hope it will wean you away from the idea-sphere. This book is about a genuine, real thing you can touch. The difference between an idea and a thing you can touch was illustrated tragically to me years ago when a friend of mine, on LSD, thought he was pulling the trigger of a water pistol aimed at his temple but it was a loaded Colt .45. Ideas have their validity, but they're no match for reality. Reality overrules every time. That's why these days I find it so hard to appreciate fiction. So much of what passes for reality is fiction enough!

The reality of this book is: IF YOU DON'T LIKE WHAT'S HAPPENING IN YOUR LIFE, YOU CAN FIX IT. You can fix it without cheating anyone, without counselling with experts, without subscribing to any newsletter that keeps you posted on inside info, without writing Washington or getting involved in politics, without organizing, and without spending a penny unless you choose to.

And a miracle will happen: as you fix what's wrong in your OWN life, you'll automatically be fixing what's wrong with America's well-being. Instantly you'll begin claiming your little-known and completely legal economic rights, good for hundreds even thousands of extra dollars in your family treasury, and not applying to government for it, either! Couldn't you use some extra cash in these raw times? The law provides benefits for you, regardless of your age, condition, financial status, sex, or whatever. Benefits to help you survive the ups and downs and starts and jolts of this fluctuating economy. But if you continue swirling about in the weightlessness of ideas you'll never know how to claim these benefits. No, to experience THIS miracle, you must be down to earth.

I've shown this manuscript to people who can be counted on for merciless feedback. Any one of them would have halted publication simply by responding with faint praise. But the unanimous verdict seems to be "At last, a book that describes the problem and then gives a DIRECT, QUICK, NATURAL SOLUTION." I believe in direct quick, natural solutions. I believe that when you have a mosquito bite, you should scratch it, not take Milk of Magnesia. Trying to solve one's own personal financial dilemma by appealing to the idea-sphere — government, federations, organizations, advisors, financial planners, experts — is submitting to surgery for that mosquito bite. A sad, tragic, waste of time, resources, and happiness.

I hope judges and mayors and court clerks, and all levels of government employees will read this little book, because it was written as much for them as for people in the private sector. I hope bankers and reporters and small businessmen and schoolteachers will read it. And attorneys, who call themselves our guardians of the law. And church folks will read it, too, because after all God is the foundation of all miracles, including the restoration of a happy America. I cannot describe how vividly God progressed in me, from an idea to a touchable reality, as this book developed. Perhaps you will sense it as you read on.

Dream worlds are hard to leave. Even *painful* dream worlds are hard to leave. They're especially hard to leave when the dream makers tell us that leaving the dream world will be catastrophic. Many people actually *prefer* the idea-sphere to reality, not caring that they are denying their whole selves pleasures of incredible intensity, pleasures and abilities truly "undreamed of". These people, and they are among out most respected citizens, are fully trained to believe in the life broadcast in the idea-sphere, and they believe it can't get much better than it is. They'll never come around to reality until they must.

This little book can only switch on the lights for people who are already tossing and turning under a terrifying yet fascinating nightmare. Suddenly, you bolt awake and there are your walls, the pictures, the lamps, the quilt, the soft breathing of your family. What had been twisting your body and mind was nothing but ideas, and they scamper away as soon as you open your eyes to the glowing warmth of the real world.

We don't need to restore the American Dream; we need to *wake up from it.*

"It is historically true that no order of society ever perishes, save by its own hand."

2
The Only Cause Of Inflation

THERE IS only one cause of inflation. There can only be one cause of inflation. That cause is *artificial money*. Artificial money gets its value from what it *represents*. Real money gets its value from what it *is*, from its rarity, its utility, its uniformity, and its durability.

In a closed society artificial money is highly acceptable. Polynesian tribesmen have used shells, beads, and stones in the same way gamblers in the casinos of Las Vegas and Atlantic City use plastic poker chips: they're fine within their specific circle, but when a gambler and a Polynesian do business together, the Polynesian won't take poker chips and the gambler won't take shells, beads, and stones. Something more "universal" has to be used as their medium of exchange.

The universal medium of exchange between differing tribal systems since 3600 B.C. has been gold or gold and silver. I saw a recent piece of economic research showing that 99.6 per cent of the people on this planet esteem gold above all else as a medium of exchange. International commerce has never been possible without gold and silver and never will be.

How gold and silver gets into the monetary system of countries is best expressed in the United States Coinage Act of 1792, which is still in effect today:

> SECTION 14. *And be it further enacted,* That it shall be lawful for any person to bring to the mint gold and silver bullion, in order to their being coined; and that

the bullion so brought shall be there assayed and coined as speedily as may be after the receipt thereof, and that free of expense to the person or persons by whom the same shall have been brought. And as soon as the said bullion shall have been coined, the person or persons by whom the same shall have been delivered, shall upon demand receive in lieu thereof coins of the same species of bullion which shall have been so delivered, weight for weight, of the pure gold or pure silver therein contained: *Provided nevertheless,* That it shall be at the mutual option of the party or parties bringing such bullion, and of the director of the said mint, to make an immediate exchange of coins for standard bullion, with a deduction of one half per cent from the weight of the pure gold, or pure silver contained in said bullion, as an indemnification of the mint for the time which will necessarily be required for coining the said bullion, and for the advance which shall have been so made in coins.

Artificial money is introduced into gold-and-silver systems as bills of credit, certificates, notes, or I.O.U.s. Artificial money explains its usefulness this way: "Why lug around all that gold and silver? Why not let your government or your bank keep your gold and silver for you, and in return we'll issue you these lovely paper certificates which are much easier to transport? Of course it goes without saying that if you ever want your gold and silver back, all you need do is present the paper and we'll return your money to you."

Imagine the temptation of having a vault full of the people's gold and silver while the people are perfectly happy to use paper! At some point, any thinking custodian is going to say, "No one is asking for his gold and silver to be redeemed. Everyone considers paper to be money now. Paper is easier to print than gold is to dig out of the mine. Hmmmm. By printing up paper notes, I can actually MAKE money!"

And so, gradually, you print up more bills of credit than there is gold and silver to back them. A few people notice that certain items are more expensive this year than last, but that could be due to demand for the items, or a shortage. No big worry. Nobody complains, except a few prophets of doom who can be written off as crackpots.

You grow delirious with joy as time passes. You buy a beautiful 10-acre lot and build a mansion on it, paying with paper you printed, that everyone's delighted to accept. How can you help but feel confident and somewhat self-important? This is the life! You throw a lot of cocktail parties.

Within a few years, there is so much paper in circulation that gold and silver can now be denounced as old fashioned: who uses it anymore? People find gold and silver money in coin shops and it's way overpriced. Relics of the past. (*It's interesting to note that gold and silver coin are routinely called "relics of the past" by friends of artificial money, and have been so-called since . . . well, the remotest past*).

To explain rising prices and sudden layoffs, complicated formulae appear from "institutes of economic studies," formulae that attempt to build a "value index" according to "national energy" and the "gross national product." These formulae are understood only by their creators, and each institute has a set of creators who feel their formulae are superior to others. Doctorate degrees and lofty distinctions are accorded these people, and they write textbooks that train young minds.

You give a big grant to one of these institutes for further studies and in the bargain get a nice tax deduction.

Loss of the currency's purchasing power is called "the rising cost of living" rather than "embezzlement." (*What does an embezzler do but increase his victim's cost of living?*)

As individual fortunes dwindle and the people clamor for relief and leadership, government and civilian spokesmen condemn "government spending" as the chief cause of inflation. "Government," much a creature of the idea-sphere as "Uncle Sam," makes an ideal whipping boy because it can be whipped indefinitely and not break or die. In fact, as the past 20 or so years testify, the more government is whipped, the more brutishly powerful it grows.

Constitutional amendments that would limit federal spending are proposed and there is much verbiage and correspondence on this. Relief and leadership are just over the horizon, the people are led to believe. As you crank out more paper, you ask the people to have a little hope and faith, and while they're at it, cut way back on their simplest pleasures. *Sacrifice,* and rest assured that our most distinguished economists are working overtime with government to try to hammer out a solution to this most pressing, most intricate problem.

What our most brilliant economists and articulate statesmen neglect to mention is that the solution to inflation is already clearly contained in the United States Constitution.

Yes. It's right there, just waiting to be acted upon. What you won't hear on radio or TV (*surely you know how the banks and government regulations make the media walk the thin line of fear)* is that YOU, personally, YOU have more power than your senators, your representatives, your state officials, even more power than the President of the United States himself when it comes to restoring economic well-being to your country. And you can start IMMEDIATELY, whenever you get ready to.

You won't have to send the first telegram or email to your congressman. You won't have to march in protest. You won't even have to organize. There'll be no long wait for a Supreme Court decision. The "right candidate" won't have to get elected. You won't really have to do anything, in fact, except *decline to break the law.* So you have nothing to risk. Whoever got into trouble for declining to break the law?

To use your power, you'll need to know a little about where American money comes from. And where *your* power comes from. And, of course, you'll need to know about the law you're going to decline to break. Some people get fidgety when "law" is brought up in a discussion of social action, so perhaps you'd enjoy being reassured that your power is well-insulated, that you won't get into any trouble when you wield it.

We'll start, then with the assurance.

"We hold these Truths to be self-evident, that all Men are created equal, that they are endowed by their Creator with certain unalienable Rights, that among these are Life, Liberty, and the Pursuit of Happiness — That to secure these Rights, Governments are instituted among Men, deriving their just powers from the Consent of the Governed, that whenever any form of Government becomes destructive of these Ends, it is the Right of the People to alter or to abolish it."

3

The Right to Alter, Reform, or Abolish

KNOWLEDGEABLE lawyers tell me that there is no finer state constitution than Tennessee's. The very first article in this state's Constitution is a Declaration of Rights, which means that the authors put the people first, above all else. The first section of Article 1 puts both state and local governments firmly under the control of you and me.

> *All power is inherent in the people, and all free governments are founded on their authority, and instituted for their peace, safety, and happiness.*

This is certainly a comforting statement and describes the relationship of the people to government, but what if the government were to gradually begin *limiting* the peace, safety, and happiness of the people? Is there something the people can do in that case? Yes. The very next clause in Article 1 Section 1 spells it out in no uncertain terms:

> *For the advancement of those ends, they have, at all times, an unalienable and indefeasible right to alter, reform, or abolish the government in such manner as they may think proper.*

Now, if you know of a stronger guarantee of human liberty than those words, please show it to me. Not even the United States Constitution assures the individual such awesome power with such bold expression. "In such manner as they may think proper" preserves the right to *revolt in violence* if you think it proper, it even allows you to be wrong in the manner you choose to reform, abolish or alter the government.

Happily, the lawful remedy for economic disaster presented here does not call for violence. But it does call for a slight alteration in state governmental practice. Does knowing that your Constitution immunizes you from punishment for altering your government, does knowing this allay any fears you might have had that you could get into trouble for flexing your power in the face of officials? It sure did for me, and I hope it does for you. If you're not a Tennessean, your state constitution assures you the implied right to alter your government lawfully as well, for reasons you'll soon discover as you read on.

There's even further insulation against trouble. In the Tennessee Constitution (*and all state constitutions*) there is a requirement that all officials authorized by the Constitution — all elected or appointed persons, state and local — "take an oath to support the Constitution of this State, and of the United States." What this means is that every judge, legislator, mayor, commissioner, agent, clerk, governor, law officer, sheriff — everyone of authority in state and local government must swear or affirm to support the people's "unalienable and indefeasible right to alter, reform, or abolish the government in such manner as they may think proper." Not only must they allow you to reform, alter, or abolish, they must also support you in doing so!

Did you know you had so much power over those smart, influential dignitaries you read about in the newspapers and see on TV? Perhaps you should pause a moment and let it all sink in: all government officials are your servants, and if you think they are not doing their job well, you can deal with them in such manner (*humane, of course*) as you may think proper. *Guaranteed by law.*

Public servants, of course, know of the power you reserve over them before they take their oath. If the terms frighten them, they can always find work elsewhere. Certainly no one forces any civilian to join government. They're there of their own free will. Their awareness of your power explains why so many state and local government employees are so congenial and cooperative. They are aware that at the slightest provocation you can arise with your awesome and *utterly lawful* power and humiliate them. You can put them out of a job if they in any way abridge your "peace, safety, and happiness."

It requires genuine dedication and unselfishness to be a good public servant, and I'm happy to say that most of my friends in government fit that description to a tee.

"It is apparent from the whole context of the Constitution as well as the history of the times which gave birth to it, that it was the purpose of the Convention to establish a currency consisting of the precious metals. These were adopted by a permanent rule excluding the use of a perishable medium of exchange, such as of certain agricultural commodities recognized by the statutes of some States as tender for debts, or the still more pernicious expedient of paper Currency."

4
A Favorable Crisis for Crushing Paper Money

VIRTUALLY all social crises are caused and cured by money. The Constitution of the United States, which is the Supreme Law of the Land, was drafted in order to relieve the country of what George Washington dismally reported was "anarchy and confusion." The anarchy and confusion was brought about by the people's inability to produce, buy, sell, and work for units of money with value that could be counted on. The money had no substance. You would agree to produce a chair for a man at a price, but by the time you finished and got paid, the money you received would not be worth half what it was worth when you began. Therefore, people would not agree to assist one another. Bad contracts. Bickering. Bad feelings. Suspicion. Fixed paralysis.

Was George Washington less affected by inflation than you and I? The definitive constitutional historian George Bancroft portrays the father of our country as an ordinary citizen harried by overdue bills — always a symptom of paper money disease:

> In 1786, "his income, uncertain in its amount, was not sufficient to meet his unavoidable expenses, and he became more straitened for money than he had ever been since his boyhood; so that he was even obliged to delay paying the annual bill of his physician, to put off the tax-gatherer once and again, and, what was harder, to defer his charities . . ."

Nine months before the Constitution was signed in Philadelphia, Washington wrote to General Knox: "Good God! who could have foreseen, or predicted the disorders which have arisen in these states!" We could very well be saying those same words ourselves today, you and I and our most astute statesmen, businessmen, and judicial officers, because (*to repeat*) *inflation can't be appreciated for what it is until it's felt, until it happens.*

I remember people telling me in 1969 "We're going to have a horrible inflation where a loaf of bread will cost a dollar," and I remember answering "So what? If prices go higher, government will simply print more money. No problem."

What I was pathetically ignorant of was that when bread goes from a dime to a dollar a loaf, the entire order of things tilts on its axis: government and education fatten to insolence, quality and pride of craft vanish, drug highs are celebrated in entertainments designed for families, sexual aberrations become politicized into badges of dignity, audiences delight in blood gushing from stage and screen, pornographers open shops in neighborhoods, and — all across the land — an array of broken homes, broken oaths and promises, broken laws, broken hearts, broken bodies.

Two decades ago I could say "So what?" to inflation simply because I hadn't *felt* it. Inflation as a future thing is utterly incomprehensible. "Who could have foreseen or predicted the disorders which have arisen . . ." It's precisely because we couldn't foresee its disorders that we let inflation happen to us. George Washington and the Continental Congress let it happen to them for the same reason.

The permanent antidote to inflation was arrived at in the Constitution Convention in Philadelphia.

At the drafting of the U.S. Constitution, there were many Friends of Paper Money present. On August 16, 1787, when the discussion arose on Article 1 Section 8, the proposed wording was this:

> *The legislature of the United States shall have the power to . . . coin money . . . and emit bills on the credit of the United States."*

A hot argument ensued on the power to emit bills of credit, which is another way of saying "printing paper money." Here are the actual words James Madison wrote describing the debate in his diary:

> *Mr. Morris moved to strike out "and emit bills of credit." If the United States had credit such bills would not be necessary; if they had no credit, unjust and useless.*
>
> *MADISON: "Will it not be sufficient to prohibit making them a tender? This will remove the temptation to emit them with unjust views. And promissory notes in that shape may in some emergencies be best."*
>
> *MORRIS: "Striking out the words will leave room for notes of a responsible minister which will do all the good without the mischief. The Monied interest will oppose the plan of Government, if paper emissions be not prohibited."*
>
> *COL. MASON, though he had a mortal hatred to paper money, yet as he could not foresee all emergencies, was unwilling to tie the hands of the Legislature. [Legislature = Congress].*

MR. MERCER: (A friend of paper money). "It was impolitic . . .to excite the opposition of all those who were friends to paper money."

MR. ELSEWORTH thought this was a favorable moment to shut and bar the door against paper money. The mischiefs of the various experiments which had been made, were now fresh in the public mind and had excited the disgust of all the respectable part of America. By withholding the power from the new Government more friends of influence would be gained to it than by almost anything else . . . Give the Government credit, and other resources will offer. The power may do harm, never good.

*MR. WILSON: "It will have a most salutary influence on the credit of the United States to remove the possibility of paper money. This **experiment** can never succeed whilst its mischiefs are remembered, and as long as it can be resorted to, it will be a bar to other resources."*

MR. READ thought the words, if not struck out, would be as alarming as the mark of the Beast in Revelation.

MR. LANGDON had rather reject the whole plan than retain the three words "and emit bills."

— The motion for striking out carried.

George Bancroft writes:

James Madison left his testimony that "the pretext for a paper currency, and particularly for making the bills a tender, either for public or private debts, was cut off. This is the interpretation of the clause, made at the time of its adoption alike by its authors and by its opponents, accepted by all the statesmen of that age, not open to dispute because too clear for argument, and never disputed so long as any one man who took part in framing the constitution remained alive.

Thus, as inflation gnawed painfully on their fortunes, our forefathers deliberately and conclusively forbade Congress the power to emit bills of credit, empowering Congress only *to coin money and regulate its value.*
The door to paper money was shut but not locked. For although Congress was not given the power to print money, it was not *denied* the power to *borrow* money. Thus, the possibility still remained that Congress' creditor, its banker, might lend congress money and circulate **the I.O.U.s of Congress** as currency. Congress would *not* be emitting bills of credit, its banker would instead.
On August 28, Article 1 Section 10 was debated. The standing version was worded this way:

"No state shall coin money; nor grant letters of marque and reprisal; nor enter into any Treaty, alliance, or confederation; nor grant any title of nobility."

The remarks on Article 1 Section 10 were short and sweet. Here is Madison's account of them:
*MR. WILSON & MR. SHERMAN moved to insert after the words "coin money" the words **"nor emit bills of credit, nor make any thing but gold and silver coin a tender in payment of debts"** making these prohibitions absolute, instead of making the measures allowable with the consent of the Legislature of the U.S.*
*MR. SHERMAN thought this **a favourable crisis for crushing paper money**. If the consent of the Legislature could authorize emissions of it, the friends*

of paper money would make every exertion to get into the Legislature in order to licence it.

Mr. Wilson's and Sherman's motion was quickly agreed to and became the supreme Law of the Land. Is there any doubt that Article 1 Section 10 *absolutely prohibited paper money,* crushing it forever, locking the door in its face? The system was, and is, simply ingenious. *With Section 8, Congress was denied the power to print money. But in order to keep the "friends of paper money" from obtaining the "licence" to monetize United States debt, Section 10 prohibited the states from declaring irredeemable paper (or anything other than gold and silver coin) to be a tender in payment of debts.*

If you don't quite understand the foregoing sentences, and the following one as well, read and reread them until you do; they're the most important sentences in this book. Article 1 Section 10's most salient point is this:

NO STATE SHALL MAKE ANY THING BUT GOLD AND SILVER COIN A TENDER IN PAYMENT OF D   E   B   T   S   .

Contemporary verbal sketches of Roger Sherman, the delegate from Connecticut who was the author of those monumental **17 words,** depict him as a learned man, steeped in historical knowledge but immensely bashful due to stammering speech and physical awkwardness. He was born in 1721 in Massachusetts, and learned farming and shoemaking from his father. His formal education consisted of just a few years in his youth; he filled out the rest independently. He published almanacs based on his own astronomical calculations, and included both original and classical poetry. He operated his own general store. At the age of 31 he wrote a searing indictment of paper money, *A Caveat Against injustice: or, and Enquiry Into the Evil Consequences of a Fluctuating Medium of Exchange.* In 1766, at the age of 45, Roger Sherman was elected Judge of the Superior Court in New Haven, Connecticut, serving that office with distinction until 1788.

He was the only American to sign all four historic documents: the Continental Association of 1774, the Declaration of Independence of 1776, the Articles of Confederation, and the United States Constitution. Renowned for his high intelligence and unswerving honesty, Roger Sherman was described by John Adams to be "as honest as an angel and as firm in the cause of American independence as Mount Atlas."

In 1791 he was elected to the United States Senate, where he served until his death in 1793. This quiet, humble, awkward man who farmed, educated himself, worked with his hands and his mind making shoes and poetry, making astronomical and economic calculations, making law and justice, is completely unknown to all but a handful of early American historians. Yet, if Judge Sherman hadn't stood up that hot August afternoon in Philadelphia and uttered **Article 1 Section 10,** America would have been an endless series of banana republics, regime after regime printing itself out of existence.

Thank God we're rediscovering those **17 words** at this late date, hopefully in time to avert the tragedy that is sure to envelop us if we choose to remain blind to them.

Those 17 words are the American Reality.

Thomas Jefferson paid Judge Sherman the most earnest and valuable compliment: "Roger Sherman was a man who never said a foolish thing in his life."

"I place economy among the first and most important virtues, and public debt as the greatest of dangers to be feared . . . We must not let our rulers load us with perpetual debt. We must make our choice between economy and liberty, or profusion and servitude . . . The same prudence which in private life would forbid our paying money for unexplained projects, forbids it in the disposition of public money. We are endeavoring to reduce the government to the practice of rigid economy to avoid burdening the people."

5
Tranquility, Prosperity & Relief

IT TOOK a little more than four months to write the U.S. Constitution, and almost a year for the states to ratify it. Then another year for the government to be set up. The most immediate relief brought about by the Constitution was economic. The cause of this economic relief was **Article 1 Section 10,** which prohibited the states from enforcing payment in anything but gold and silver coin. If people wanted to, they could make deals using for exchange cattle, paper money, real estate, tobacco, chickens, peanuts — *any thing* they could agree on. But when it came to the state's participation in anyone's economic life, such as enforcing fines, taxes, judgements, etc., the terms were spelled out quite clearly and absolutely in **Article 1 Section 10.** Nothing but gold and silver coin; no THING other than that.

Did putting America on a sound money basis hurt anyone? Did it cause a disastrous economic upheaval? Did it throw bankers into bankruptcy, businessmen out of business, government employees out into the cold? The best source of information on this should be none other than George Washington himself, who was a businessman, bureaucrat, farmer, banker, legislator, and military man, among other things. This excerpt is from a letter he wrote to his good friend, the Marquis de LaFayette, dated June 3, 1790, less than a year after the ratification of the Constitution. It shows quite dramatically what happens when an economy goes from paper money to gold and silver coin:

You have doubtless been informed, from time to time, of the happy progress of our affairs. The principal difficulties seem in a great measure to have been surmounted. Our revenues have been considerably more productive than it was imagined they would be. I mention this to show the spirit of enterprise that prevails.

How about that! Revenues "more productive than it was imagined they would be." Couldn't *we* use some "considerable more productive revenues" and some "spirit of enterprise" these days? All it takes is gold and silver coin.

The public record is filled with jubilant reports of the effects of the Constitution's monetary system. The December 16, 1789 edition of *The Pennsylvania Gazette* exclaimed:

Since the federal constitution has removed all danger of our having a paper tender, our trade is advanced fifty per cent. Our monied people can trust their case abroad, and have brought their coin into circulation.

Again, Washington wrote to LaFayette, on March 19, 1792.

Our country, my dear sir, is fast progressing in its political importance and social happiness.

On July 19, 1791, in a letter to Catherine Macaulay Graham, Washington wrote:

The United States enjoys a sense of prosperity and

tranquility under the new government that could hardly have been hoped for.

And finally, on July 20, 1791, Washington wrote with glowing exuberance to David Humphreys:

Tranquility reigns among the people with that disposition towards the general government which is likely to preserve it. Our public credit stands on that high ground which three years ago it would have been considered as a species of madness to have foretold.

In other words, Washington was saying "If anyone had predicted that our economic and social problems could have been solved by simply making nothing but gold and silver coin our money, he would have been called crazy."

Like so many people today, Washington had originally felt that the "anarchy and confusion" was being caused by a great host of demons, paper money being just one of them. What he didn't realize until after the ratification was that irredeemable paper money had been the sole creator of those demons. When it vanished, the demons vanished.

Since paper money requires no labor to exist, it rewards people who perform no labor. Non-working people who receive rewards have an exaggerated sense of their worth. "Non-work" includes vacuum-work. "Vacuum-work" is work performed in an area where there's no real demand for it, like dumb projects (*Jefferson called them "unexplained projects"*). Government rewards vacuum-work highly, either directly or through tax advantages to persons who subsidize vacuum-work.

When non-working people receive rewards for non-work, it turns working people against their own jobs. Reward for non-work makes working people consider the advantages of not working. Non-work is a failure to demonstrate one's capabilities as a human being. Since non-work is a statement that one is not willing directly to assist humanity, you can be sure that the rewards from non-work will be spent on things that belittle and harm humanity. Instead of contribution to humanity, the rewarded non-worker commits himself to the source of his reward, that incorporation of humanity called government.

With each allegiance from rewarded non-workers and from workers doing things for which there is no real demand, a government elected by the people can construct an entire block of non-workers and vacuum workers and grant it unlimited power over real workers. A rewarded non-worker is a self-declared enemy of his fellow man, conspiring with his government to create chaos, bloodshed, injustice, corruption, hardship, and heartbreak. It was so in Washington's time and it is so in ours. It's always been so.

Inflation turns people into weightless balloons, all hollow inside, filled with hot air. Solid substance has been removed. We "float" aloft, just like our money. Our skin is blown up all out of proportion, and we have nothing to offer but appearance. Appearance and hype are everything, just like the money. Our inner selves are just vacant air. Our outer selves are what we are: a shell, skin. This must have been the condition T.S. Eliot was describing with his image of "hollow men." In every inflation that has ever occurred, the people develop an obsession for external things: sports; violence; pornography; and especially fashion and gesture. These are the ornaments of tyranny.

No historian can show you a tryanny founded on a free-flowing money based on gold and silver coin, because tyranny in history has resulted from the debasement (de-base = removing the basis of value) of the people's gold and silver money.

With a sense of forgiveness, I must mention here that the actual legislators of money debasement, in our own and other countries, are typically persons operating in good faith who simply don't know what they're doing. We allow them to debase our money because *we* don't know what *we*'re doing, either. Remember, inflation is like pain: it can't be felt until it's experienced. This is why deadly inflations are almost always spaced a couple of generations apart.

All the horrors of the managed paper economy were snuffed out in 1789 by **Article 1 Section 10,** right before George Washington's astonished eyes. It put non-workers to work and gave them value, infused them with "a spirit of enterprise." Painlessly, miraculously, it restored sanity and purpose to a badly shaken population. The wonderful thing about an economy based on gold and silver is that it lets you know precisely what your fiscal worth is. It enables you to plan ahead, to feel proud of yourself and your work. Bad neurotic habits can break of themselves when you know how valuable you are.

Gold and silver stops politicians from creating floods of money to spend on programs that encourage non- and vacuum-work, it stops banks from creating loans out of thin air to underwrite dumb projects, it . . . here I am in the middle of a sales pitch. Why should I ask anyone to please, let's start using a gold and silver monetary base in the United States of America? This is as stupid as begging Congress to give women the right to vote. Women already have the right to vote, and WE ALREADY HAVE A GOLD AND SILVER MONETARY BASE IN THE UNITED STATES! Judge Roger Sherman, God bless his soul, saw to that on August 28, 1787, in a **17 word law** that has never been repealed, rescinded, or amended in any way whatsoever!

NO STATE SHALL MAKE ANY THING BUT GOLD AND SILVER COIN A TENDER IN PAYMENT OF DEBTS.

If we *already* have a gold and silver monetary base, why then do we not have gold and silver coinage in circulation? What happened to the law?

Are we being governed by a bunch of criminals?

"*Those who create and issue money and credit direct the policies of government and hold in the hollow of their hands the destiny of the people.*"

"*In the United States today we have in effect two governments . . . We have the duly constituted Government . . . Then we have an independent, uncontrolled and uncoordinated government in the Federal Reserve System, operating the money powers which are reserved to Congress by the Constitution.*"

"*A pro-International Monetary Fund Seminar of eminent economists couldn't agree on what 'money' is or how banks create it.*"

6
Weavers of "The American Dream"
The Friends of Paper Money

IT'S a matter of history that in 1913, the Friends of Paper Money gained a real stronghold on the American economic system through the Federal Reserve Act. In the passage of that Act, a small group of world bankers with a long and carefully-guarded, very private history of manipulating the affairs of rulers "got into the Legislature," just as Roger Sherman feared they would, and obtained "licence" to print money.

There's nothing in the Constitution to prevent Congress from contracting with a private corporation for the management of a popular currency. *The Federal Reserve is a private corporation?* Yes. Super-private. Its voting stockholders are kept in secret; they're known to no one, not even the President of the United States. The Federal Reserve System is not part of the U.S. Government, and has never been audited by the General Accounting Office or any government agency. Of course, it *seems* to be an official department, with the President appointing some directors and such, but the Federal Reserve is completely autonomous. Asked, "Do you approve of the latest credit-tightening moves," Treasury Secretary David M. Kennedy answered in *U.S. News & World Report,* May 5, 1969, "It's not my job to approve or disapprove. It is the action of the Federal Reserve."

The chief architect of the Federal Reserve System was a world banker of extraordinary ability, Paul

Monitz Warburg, who had come to this country from Germany in 1902. He was born an heir to the powerful Fankfurt banking house of M.N. Warburg & Company. Reading Paul Warburg's speeches on money feels like dipping your hand into a bucket of diamonds: his words are winningly precise, hard, correct. I admire him without reservation. It would take nothing less than a man of Mr. Warburg's brilliance to sell the concept of central banking to the discerning American people. Here's a sample of his salesmanship, from an address he gave at Columbia University in 1907:

In order to conserve the interests of the public, banks should be permitted, within certain limitations with respect to capital, to issue circulating notes. They should be redeemable (for gold and silver coins) over a bank's counter, at the United States Treasury, and at convenient points throughout the country, thereby maintaining the notes at par throughout the country.

While I believe that such a currency can be successfully applied to the sixty-five hundred banks now in existence, yet judged from an historical and scientific standpoint, the currency system of a country can best be administered through the instrumentality of a central bank of issue.

With a pronounced trend in favor of centralization, with the popular and growing demand that all corporations, national in their scope and character, be regulated by the national government, is it not logical and fair to assume that public sentiment will presently demand that the government's receipts and disbursements shall be made through a central bank?
— The Currency Problem, Columbia University Press, 1908, p.50.

If I had been present at that lecture, I probably

would have cheered Mr. Warburg on. His words plainly make sense. Who could have foreseen that between 1923 and 1929, the Federal Reserve would print up a *62 per cent inflation* and then suddenly stop, whiplashing the country into the crash of 1929, followed by a numbing depression that lasted more than ten years? Who could have foreseen all the stops and starts which have plagued our economy since the creation of the Federal Reserve? Who could have predicted the wars, the hardships, the moral decay, the internal division? Who could have predicted that the national debt would have risen from one billion dollars in 1913 to *multi-trillions* in our present time? And who pays off that debt? You and your kids.

Well, is the Federal Reserve a giant, sinister conspiracy out to destroy and/or enslave us; a menacing foe against which we are powerless? Of course not. Federal Reserve people are nice folks, good members of their communities. They go to church, play golf, contribute to worthwhile charities just as you may do. And like most people in business, they have a product to sell. To sell this product, they have to overcome customer resistance.

Like "McDonald's" or "The 10 O'Clock News" or "Pepsi-Cola" or the "Avon" lady down the street, the Federal Reserve operates *by staking a claim on your imagination.* They do everything within the law to get you to believe in their product. The Federal Reserve exists because *you let it exist.* You patronize its nationwide franchises, the friendly banks opening onto Main Street U.S.A. You believe in the Federal Reserve just as you believe in Pepsi-Cola or your insurance man, and that's why irredeemable paper notes have become the money you use, the money you're finding ever more difficult to keep track of and maintain.

Since the Federal Reserve, like a dream, exists because you believe in it, it can cease to exist as soon as you stop believing in it. That's the way the idea-sphere works. The 10 O'Clock News surrenders its claim on you the instant you turn off your TV. Moreover, most of the people at the top of the Federal Reserve *know* that they owe their livelihood to your credence in them, and that once you decide that their product is not what it's cracked up to be, you can make them improve it.

But as long as you are willing to reduce your circumstances in order to make room for greater floods of paper and digital "money supply," the people at the Federal Reserve and their member banks *really see no need to improve their product.*

As long as you're willing to believe that the cause of inflation is government spending or OPEC oil or the "Crisis in the Middle East" or wherever, as long as you're willing to get out and "politik" for the candidate whom you think will stop inflation (*has any candidate ever licked inflation upon election?*), as long as you think the President's "inflation Fighter" (*usually a Federal Reserve director or governor or intimate*) can lick inflation, as long as you're willing to gripe and complain and bicker with your grocer and the power company and your gas pump owner about what they're charging you, as long as you're content to blow smoke and howl at the moon . . . the Friends of Paper Money have no reason to lift a finger to change things.

. . . Except to raise interest rates, which penalizes

you more and enables them to increase their grasp on your purse-strings several notches while you're trying to figure out why you got laid off.

"He has combined with others to subject us to a Jurisdiction foreign to our Constitution, and unacknowledged by our laws."

"An inefficient, unemployed, disorganized Europe is an extant example of how much man can suffer and how far society can decay. Economic privation proceeds by easy stages, and so long as men suffer it patiently the outside world cares little. Physical efficiency and resistance to disease slowly diminish, but life proceeds somehow, until the limit of human endurance is reached at the last and counsels of despair and madness stir the sufferers from the lethargy which precedes the crisis. Then man shakes himself and the bonds of custom are loosed. The power of ideas is sovereign, and he listens to whatever instruction of hope, illusion, or revenge is carried to him on the air."

7

Paul's Brother Max

ACROSS the Atlantic, the German federal reserve —
a central bank of issue call the *Reichsbank* — performed an experiment in artificial money that devas-
tated the German people, 1916-1923. Pearl S. Buck
wrote a book about it with Erna von Pustau called
How It Happens. Genocide by paper flood is docu-
mented in this book with dramatic eye-witness vivid-
ness.

In the beginning days, as the *Reichsbank* started
issuing paper credit out of thin air, the German press
excitedly called inflation "the miracle of German industry!" No wonder. Everybody had money and credit,
just like in America in the roaring 1920's. But soon the
dream turned nightmarish. Recalling her brother's
remarks about his normally thrifty wife, Frau von Pustau
describes Germany around 1919:

> *Robert first looked puzzled, then he said to me, "You
> know, Hilde is just how women ought to be. But it's
> madness to save nowadays." Saving is the very source
> of the wealth and health of a sound nation. We were
> on our way to becoming a crazy, a neurotic, a mad
> nation.*

The press cooperated not with the struggling, suffering, people who looked to their newspapers for answers, but with the Friends of Paper Money. No attempt was made to publish or broadcast the one true
cause of inflation; to lead the people to the solution.
Unfortunately for them, the Germans had had no Roger

Sherman, no **Article 1 Section 10;** they were completely at the mercy of the *Reichsbank* and industry (*itself indebted to the Reichsbank*) and, of course, the government (*the Reichsbank's largest debtor*). Please note that the Director of the *Reichsbank* at this time was none other than Max Warburg, the brother of the Paul Warburg who created and served as a governor of America's Federal Reserve Board. Also note that during much of this period, our boys and German boys were fighting the bloodiest war in world history up to that time. Millions of people were being killed in that war.

The newspapers and radios published all kinds of tips and hints on how to live with inflation, buying cheaper cuts of meat, staying cold in winter, just generally reducing one's needs in the interest of "conservation" — that kind of thing, with which I'm sure you're quite familiar.

"Inflation is a thing which has slipped out of control of everyone," the newspapers lamented. As times grew worse, the media began blaming "foreigners," gold speculators, and gold hoarders. Of course, hoarding gold is just about the *only* defense anyone has against inflation. Even in the last frantic days, the press was still terming inflation "a catastrophe of nature." Do you see any similarities between the media then and now?

Frau von Pustau says:

By the end of the year my allowance and all the money I earned were not worth one cup of coffee. You could go to the baker in the morning and buy two rolls for 20 marks; but go there in the afternoon, and the same two rolls would cost 25 marks. The baker didn't know how it happened. His customers didn't now how it happened. It had somehow to do with the dollar, somehow to do with the stock exchange — and somehow, maybe, to do with the Jews.

Confusion, mass ignorance, debates flaming from all sides, complicated solutions proposed by experts: "All these technical questions made it difficult for anybody to understand for a long time what was happening," Frau von Pustau says. And while no one was understanding, the Friends of Paper Money were pocketing more and more of the people's property. She recalls:

When Father came back from vacation, he said that the workers had discovered the "trick of inflation," which was to figure the value of money in gold. Time and again, the workers struck for the "adjustment of their wages," paid daily in exact accordance with the daily mark devaluation.

Those who quickly converted to gold were able to survive the inflation with their resources reasonably intact. "Quickly converting to gold" is but one step below having a redeemable currency. For those who remained ignorant of the "trick of inflation," says Frau von Pustau, "life was madness, nightmare, desperation, chaos."

Finally, out of the chaos came the cure. But the cure became a political game, a long, drawn out affair that lasted nearly six months as the various factions in government and business jockeyed for position to see who would be given credit for bringing about the cure. Says Frau von Pustau:

The government struggled hard to restore the gold

standard. But the Minister of Finance was the social-
ist, Helferding. Big business was ready now to re-
store the gold standard, but the whole clique, includ-
ing the agriculture, peasants, and Junkers wanted to
be given credit for restoring sound and solid money.
While this struggle went on, chaos increased.

And prostitution and suicide and every kind of street crime imaginable. Even *un*imaginable. It got so bad, according to Frau von Pustau, that chunks of meat were butchered from the flanks of horses standing at rest in front of their wagons and were either sold or eaten on the spot.

At length, with a loaf of bread costing billions of marks, the currency was made redeemable in gold coin and instantly the stormy sea calmed. But enormous damage had been done, both past and future for the "honor" of restoring a sound mark was given to Dr. Hjalmar Schacht, who was skyrocketed by the media to national heroism, fame and adulation because of his "accomplishment." Anyone Dr. Schacht associated with would be accorded great public esteem, because he had "rescued Germany." It's now history that Dr. Schacht chose to associate himself with Adolf Hitler, becoming the Fuhrer's chief economic advisor.

"The same monetary system that was established on April 2, 1792, is in effect today."

"The terms 'lawful money' and 'lawful money of the United States' shall be construed to mean gold or silver coin of the United States."
— UNITED STATES CODE 152

"All coins and currencies of the United States (including Federal Reserve notes and circulating notes of the Federal Reserve banks and national banking associations), regardless of when coined or issued, shall be legal tender for all debts, public and private, public charges, taxes, duties, and dues."
— 31 UNITED STATES CODE 392

8
Is Dream Money Lawful Money?

THIS may surprise you, but Congress has never declared Federal Reserve notes to be a legal tender in payment of debts. Doubt me? Look at you currency: ". . . LEGAL TENDER FOR ALL DEBTS PUBLIC AND PRIVATE." The word "FOR" is used rather than "IN PAYMENT OF." Was this just accidental? No. It is well-settled in the courts that lawmakers are presumed to have selected each word that makes up a statute carefully and deliberately, lest the statute be considered "void for vagueness." We can be sure, then, that when Congress chose NOT to use "IN PAYMENT OF," it did so for a good reason, that good reason being the hard fact that in the eyes of American jurisprudence **no debt can be paid in full unless paid in gold and silver that has been coined and regulated in value by Congress via Article 1 Sections 8 and 10.**

About all a Federal Reserve note can legally do is wipe out one debt and replace it with *itself,* another debt, a note that promises nothing. If anything's been *paid,* the payment occurs only in the minds of the parties — in the idea-sphere — not in the real world.

It's important for you to mark well that Federal Reserve notes are *NOT your government's money.* They bear the likeness of our presidents, they bear the signatures of our Treasurer and the Secretary of the Treasury, They bear beautiful engravings of our most sacred political monuments, and even — since the late 1950's — the pious religious motto "In God we Trust," *but they are not your government's money.* So when you revile American Dream Money, you're in no way insulting your government. Federal Reserve paper is not lawful money; not government money. It is the scrip of a private, for-profit corporation partly owned by your local banker. Whether it's a $100 bill or a $1 bill, a Federal Reserve note is intrinsically worth only about two cents. Its extrinsic worth is whatever it will buy from day to day in the marketplace, just like the 1916-1923 German mark.

Is this any kind of money for a stable country to have?

Between 1913 and 1963 (*fifty years*), the Federal Reserve promised redeemability in lawful money on their notes. But in 1963, they began issuing notes *minus* the redeemability promise. This enabled your banker to issue you a note that said "In God We Trust" in exchange for your silver dollar, without his having to exchange that silver dollar back for the note. An unfair deal, you might say, but who took steps to prevent it?

Interestingly, the first 50,000,000 no-promise Federal Reserve notes were shipped out on November 26, 1963, — the day of President John F. Kennedy's funeral. A coin dealer friend of mine said "You know, they couldn't have picked a better day to catch the people of America off guard. (I wonder why?)

These days it looks like there's not enough gold and silver "to go around." That's because there's so much paper. Inflation always makes people think there's a shortage in precious metals. The reason is simple: *increased paper amounts, increase prices.*

It looks, too, as though we're "off the gold standard," as a banker told me in earnest not long ago. Both this and the "not enough" assumptions are based on pure *hear-say*. How rarely we take time to check things out! How easily we surrender our lives to *gossip!* For America to be "off the gold (*or silver*) standard," the Coinage Act of April 2, 1792, which specifies in detail how our money is to be made, would have to be rescinded or repealed by Congress. Then, a constitutional amendment permitting the states to make something other than gold and silver coin a tender in payment of debts would have to be passed and *ratified by three-fourths of the states!*

As of 2003, none of these events has happened. (God help us if they ever *should* happen).

It is the Federal Reserve's monetary system that is no longer on the gold or silver standard. In the Federal Reserve's own published statement:

> *Today, in the United States (Inc.) there are only two kinds of money in use in significant amounts — currency (paper money and coins in the pockets and purses of the public), and demand deposits (checking accounts in commercial banks). Since $1 in currency and $1 in demand deposits are freely convertible into each other at the option of a bank's customer, both are money to an equal degree. What makes these instruments acceptable at face value as "payment" of all debts? Mainly, it is the confidence people have that they will be able to exchange such money for real goods and services whenever they choose to do so. — Modern Money Mechanics, published by the Federal Reserve Bank of Chicago.*

So there you have it: *paper* and *confidence* are

the monies in which we conduct our daily commercial transactions, with our friendly banker as our perpetual middleman. But have the instruments of the Federal Reserve monetary system ever qualified to be the money in which the transactions of government must be conducted? Let's investigate.

The government is limited to a special kind of money by federal statute. For you see, in order to live up to the Constitution's promise of establishing domestic tranquillity and promoting the general welfare, the people instructed their representatives to keep all official accounts and proceedings in **"The money of account of the United States."** First legislated in the Coinage Act of 1792, this requirement is found in current law at Section 371 of Title 31 of the United States Code, which you should memorize:

31 UNITED STATES CODE

The money of account of the United States shall be expressed in dollars or units, dimes or tenths, cents or hundredths, and mills or hundred parts of a dollar, a mill the thousandth part of a dollar — and **all accounts in the public offices and all proceedings in the courts shall be kept and had in conformity to this regulation.**

Thus, it is a federal regulation that all accounts in the public offices and all proceedings in the courts must be conducted in whatever has been declared to be **"The money of account of the United States,"** this money being expressed — *or measured* — in dollars."

A dollar, therefore, is neither a coin nor a piece of paper, but simply the name of the unit by which

the value of money is *measured,* just as "quart" is the name of a unit by which *liquid* is measured. A dealer selling a car for "1500 quarts" would surely be asked "Quarts of *what?* Where, then, is the frivolity in asking about a $15 parking ticket, "Fifteen dollars of what"? (Fifteen dollars of gold or silver coin.)

When courts and public offices require you to pay in dollars, the dollars must — *by the above law* — be dollars (**units**) of **"The money of account of the United States."** Is there any doubt in your mind as to what **"The money of account of the United States"** is?

The Coinage Act of 1792 specifically declared gold and silver to be "as money in the United States." But in 1933, Congress suspended our currency's redemption in gold, and in 1968 suspended the redemption of silver certificates in silver. (In both cases, the excuse was "temporary emergency," as it always is when governments work with bankers to harvest the people's property without due process). The cumulative effect of those acts of 1933 and 1968 was this:

Congress eliminated "The money of account of the United states." from the banking system without declaring a replacement, therefore neither our courts nor our public offices are complying with 31 U.S.C. 371!

Federal Reserve notes and all those confidence building, important-looking paper instruments of Federal Reserve banking may be "money," all right, but they've never been declared to be **"The money of account of the United States,"** as gold and silver have. They may even be measured in dollars or units, but not in dollars or units of **"The money of account of the United States."**

Federal Reserve notes can be a tender *for* debts, and they may even be "lawful" money, in the sense that they've never been specifically declared *un*lawful, but they are NOT **"The money of account of the United States."** that is measured in dollars, in which "all accounts in the public offices and all the proceedings in the courts shall be kept and had. And if you doubt me, just ask any judge or lawyer or attorney general to show you legislation that disproves this fact.

Federal Reserve notes are compelling images charged with enchantment and charm, like movies and TV and comic strips and stereo and colorful pages in magazines. If you believe that they — or the bank demand deposits for which they are redeemable — are the **"The money of account of the United States"** the law requires us to pay into our government, you're living in the Land of OZ.

"*All the perplexities, confusion and distress in America arise not from defects in their constitution or confederation, nor from want of honor or virtue so much as from downright ignorance of the nature of coin, credit, and circulation.*"

"*I have studied finance and economics and international trade all my life, and now, after these recent events, I have come to the conclusion that I know nothing whatever about any of them.*"

"*We have awakened forces that nobody is at all familiar with.*"

9
Starting the Miracle;
Reducing the Ignorance Factor

SIR WILLIAM GLADSTONE called the United States Constitution, "The most wonderful work ever struck off at a given time by the intuition and purpose of man." Yet, its nature and providence are unknown — according to a survey in the Bicentennial year — to more than 90% of the American people. Ninety per cent of the American people are ignorant of a great many lawful guarantees of prosperity and happiness that are theirs simply for the asking. Amazing!

The ignorance factor is not limited to the common people; it is shared in the realms of government as well. I have interviewed many important government officials who are almost totally unaware of their rights — or anyone else's — under the very document they are sworn to support. I have had the dubious pleasure of introducing for the first time to numerous state and local officials the prohibition in Article 1 Section 10 against paper money.

When an honest official discovers that he's been taking money under state authority in violation of the Constitution and his oath, he is shocked. We act strangely under shock. One typical response I hear is "Why didn't anybody tell me this? How did this happen?

One judge told me in open court, "The state must use the currency Congress issues." This statement is wrong on two counts:

1. The Congress by law, does not tell the States what shall be the tender. The Constitution, thanks to the more knowledgeable Judge Sherman, provides that **the States shall tell Congress what the lawful tender shall be: nothing but gold and silver coin.**

2. Congress doesn't issue Federal Reserve notes, a non-governmental, private "banker's bank" issues these notes.

Thus, a man with considerable power over the economic fortunes of his peers is completely ignorant of both the natural and statutory laws of money. Again, I must repeat, it's no reflection on his moral character or intelligence or even his judicial preparedness. **The ignorance of money is deep and widespread. We are all victims of the money blackout.** The Friends of Paper Money work as hard keeping us ignorant of money as some parents work at keeping their kids believing in Santa Claus and Bunny Easter eggs.

After the initial shock, the honest public official begins to worry in the back of his mind about all this. One told me he figured that there *must* be a law somewhere that permitted the state to make paper money a tender. Otherwise, he said, "The whole damn state's crazy." When he failed to turn up any such law after weeks of looking, he experienced profound misgivings about the whole purpose of government. He even considered resigning his position. He and his colleagues who were taking and giving money in the name of the state (or municipal) government were actually perjuring their Constitutional oath of office by *accepting* paper money or by *paying* in paper money. As long as people are *willing* to contribute to their government (*or accept from it*) paper money, copper, digits, automobiles, or real estate, the government is under no moral obligation to change its ways. Any law that prohibits government from accepting contributions from its citizens or discharging its debts cheaply would be a bad law indeed.

Article 1 Section 10 doesn't prohibit the state from accepting paper money. It merely prohibits the state from declaring that things other than gold and silver coin *are lawful tender.* In other words, when the state Attorney General is asked "What does the state declare is legal tender?" he *must* answer "Gold and silver coin."

If any property or sales-tax form or citation — any bill from state or local government; even a parking or speeding ticket — is labelled "Dollars," you have the right to ask the state if it means dollars of**"The money of account of the United States,"** and if so, *what is* **"The money of account of the United States"?**

The state is not likely to answer that the instrument is not denominated in **"The money of account of the United States,"** nor is it likely to tell you what **"The money of account of the United States"** is. You'll be in a quandary.

Of course, there will be no state law declaring paper to be a tender in payment of debts. It would be an embarrassing, flagrant violation of the United States Constitution. Here's an example of how rigidly a state must adhere to Article 1 Section 10. This is a case cited in the NOTES TO DECISIONS involving Article 1 Section 10 as published in the Tennessee Code annotated:

Since nothing but gold and silver coin is a legal tender, **tender in bank notes** *of the bank of the United States to redeem land sold under execution,* **if objected to** *will not be valid, although equal to coin.*
— *Lowry v. McGhee (1835) 16 Tenn. 242.*

So there it is, still on the books in the 1980 edition, a case in which the court had no choice but to sustain a man's **objection to paper currency**, even though the currency was redeemable in gold and silver coin! You can imagine what that court would have said to **irredeemable Federal Reserve paper.**

If there is no law entitling the state to enforce payment in paper money, and if the state cannot tell you what **"The money of account of the United States"** is, you and the state have reached an impasse in your economic favor, or what the St. Louis monetary realist Amos Bruce calls a "Mexican standoff." **You'll pay as soon as they show you how you can do it.**

Yes, if you choose NOT to contribute paper money to your state and local government, you have the total BLESSING of the United States Constitution (*and the ghost of Roger Sherman who will surely be smiling down upon you from the heavens*) until paper money is made redeemable for gold and silver coin. You even have the blessing of the courts and officials of government, since *they have sworn of their own volition to support Judge Sherman's* **17 words**.

And what if some government official should come after you and bug you in any way? *You* have the protection of the law, not he. All States have official *misconduct statutes.* Here's the one for Tennessee:

TENNESSEE CODE 39-3203 Official Oppression — Penalty. — If any person, by color of his office, willfully and corruptly oppresses any person, under pretense of acting in his official capacity, he shall be punished by fine not exceeding one thousand dollars ($1,000.), or imprisonment in the county jail not exceeding one (1) year.

Now, the important words in this statute are "willfully and corruptly." This means that you must first inform the official of Article 1 Section 10, of the fact that **bank credits and Federal Reserve paper money are not gold and silver coin**, and that you know he is bound by oath to support the Constitution. Explain to him that, being part of government, he is limited to taking only **"The money of account of the United States,"** and until you know what that money is, you cannot pay lawfully and properly. You see, **you're helping him not to break the law by *educating him.*** If you wanted to be especially helpful, you might send him a copy of this book. (Thank you.) Now you've given him fair warning. If he tries to oppress you from this point onward, he is being "willful and corrupt," and all you have to do — if the District Attorney plays dead — is appear before a Grand Jury yourself, tell those taxpayers what this official did, and get him *indicted!*

Don't believe the false notion that government officials are permitted to operate corruptly and safely behind "sovereign immunity" laws. There are no sovereigns in America, except we, the people, and no government official is immune from justice if he abuses our rights. You can establish a personal fortune upon the ruins of anyone who runs roughshod over your constitutional guarantees: he who would unlawfully jeopardize your property loses his property to you, and that's what justice is all about. Here's the law:

42 UNITED STATES CODE 1983

Civil action for depravation of rights. Every person who, under color of any statute, ordinance, regulation, custom, or usage, of any State or Territory, subjects, or causes to be subjected, any citizen of the United States or other person within the jurisdiction thereof to the deprivation of any rights, privileges, or immunities secured by the Constitution and laws, shall be liable to the party injured in an action at law, suit in equity, or other proper proceeding for redress.

[. . . *Upheld by the Supreme Court:* — "*The innocent individual who is harmed by an abuse of governmental authority is assured that he will be compensated for his injury.*" — *Owen v. City of Independence, 100 S.Ct. 1398 (1980)*]

Perhaps George Bancroft's "abstract of the avowed convictions of the great statesmen and jurists who made the Constitution" will intensify the potency of Article 1 Section 10 in the minds of otherwise oppressive officials and eliminate any need for legal action. Show them Bancroft's words:

History can not name a man who has gained enduring honor by causing the issue of paper money. Wherever such paper has been employed, it has in every case thrown upon its authors the burden of exculpation under the plea of pressing necessity.

Paper money has no hold, and from its very nature it can acquire no hold on the conscience or affections of the people. It impairs all certainty of possession, and taxes none so heavily as the class who earn their scant possession by daily labor. It injures the husbandman by a twofold diminution of the exchangeable value of his harvest. It is the favorite of those who seek gain without willingness to toil; it is the deadly foe of industry. No powerful political party ever permanently rested for support on the theory that it is wise and right. No statesman has been thought well of by his kind in a succeeding generation for having been its promoter.

I have found that as soon as even the most ornery government enforcement people figure out what the issue is all about (*and you have to help them; work with them*), they automatically join your side. They HAVE to, because the Constitution is on your side. To NOT agree with you is to deplore the Constitution, and many people still consider that TREASON punishable by death..

"This constitution, and the laws made in pursuance thereof shall be the supreme law of the land; and the judges in every state shall be bound thereby, any thing in the constitution or laws of any state to the contrary notwithstanding . . . and all officers of both the United States and of the several States shall be bound by oath to support this constitution."
— *Article 6, Constitution of the United States*

"Whoever, having taken a lawful oath, shall affirm willfully, corruptly and falsely touching a matter material to the point in question, shall be guilty of perjury, and on conviction shall be imprisoned in the penitentiary."   — *Tennessee Code 3903391*

"Although important decision of abortion payments, racial quotas and the commercial use of genetic engineering attracted the most attention, the Supreme Court's 1979-80 term offered one overriding theme: The expanding right of Americans to sue the government. While seldom fodder for newspaper headlines, a citizen's power to hold government and its agents responsible for lawless actions is as essential to a republican form of government as is the power of the ballot.

10
The Proper Course
for Government

THE POSITION we recommend for state, county, and municipal officers under Constitutional Oath is this: accept paper money from all persons who tender it voluntarily, but do not attempt to enforce payment from those who raise the Constitutional objection.

This position lets you live with your conscience; it's reasonable, moral, and serves the cause of freedom. Some officials are relatively immune from economic fluctuation; cost of living raises keep them more or less comfortable in the most turbulent times. Besides, it may not be in your best interests to speak out. If you took *too* original a stand, you might suffer complicated reprisals from higher-ups. No, the key to financial liberation is properly in the hands of the *people*, the people you officials serve. Let them guide you.

If the people neglect to object to paper money, take their money.

I regret saying it, but folks who labor under the illusion that they are powerless to correct their own misery *deserve* their misery. Persons who let their *right* be intimidated by *wrong* deserve intimidation. Persons who neglect to learn the benefits and privileges guaranteed by the Supreme Law of the Land *deserve* getting fleeced. Persons who don't know the difference between gold and paper don't know the difference between reality and dreams, so let them pay for living in the idea-sphere by giving up their property to the tentacles of inflation. Let them get their satisfaction from complaining and contributing to toothless organizations.

On the other hand, persons who *know* the law and exercise their *rights* under the law are lawfully immune from enforcement of payment to any state or local agency of any amount of tender not declared to be **"The money of account of the United States."**

Now, some officers might feel the temptation to answer objections to paper tender by denominating paper debts at current gold or silver quotations so they can remain true to their oath of office.

Here's the scenario:

A Taxpayer objects to a $600 property tax assessment in paper dollars, so the official levies the tax at one ounce of gold (*say gold at that moment is $520 per ounce*) plus small silver coins to make up the remainder. This is a patently unfair: gold and silver prices on the free market fluctuate very capriciously from hour to hour. The official would be working an unlawful hardship on the objector while contributing to the erosion of the economy and his own fortunes as well, no matter *how nice* a cost-of-living raise deal he might have. The objector is *leading* you to high ground in the face of a flood. Don't *fight him!* Just go by the law.

The people — *and you too* — are entitled to a constant and dependable value of gold and silver coin, **responsibly regulated by Congress, not the free market.** That's the whole purpose of Article 1 Sections 8 and 10. The "free market," by the way, is not really a free market at all, but a handful of dignitaries who declare gold and silver prices each morning in a stately private boardroom in the District of London. Who are these gentlemen more interested in, you or themselves? If you disapproved of their mischief, how can you vote them out of office? With a Congressionally regulated gold and silver currency, you could indirectly *un*vote those representatives who tampered with the value of your money.

What all this means is that knowledgeable persons — persons who object to paper money under Article 1 Sections 8 and 10, and who insist upon paying **"The money of account of the United States"** — are immune from all taxes, fees, debts of any kind under state authority, until paper money is made redeemable in gold and silver coin. This is perfectly just. Should not obedience to law and truth contain a reward?" Isn't it fitting that economic benefits should flow abundantly to those with the knowledge and courage to do the right thing, according to the law?

History's paramount lesson is this: When tragedy gathers on the horizon, the knowers act to survive. Only the knowers survive. The knowers.

The Noahs.

Since the Constitution is intended for the observance of the judiciary as well as the other departments of government and the judges are sworn to support its provisions, the courts are not at liberty to overlook or disregard its commands, or countenance evasions thereof. It is their duty in authorized proceedings to give effect to the existing constitution and to obey all constitutional provisions, irrespective of their opinion as to the wisdom or desirability of such provisions, and irrespective of the consequences. If the Constitution prescribes one rule and the statute another and a different rule, it is the duty of the courts to declare that the Constitution, and not the statute, governs in cases before them for judgment.

— 16 American Jurisprudence 2nd

"With a firm Reliance on the Protection of divine Providence, we mutually pledge to each other our Lives, our Fortunes, and our sacred Honor."

11
Under Investigation

ONE EVENING RECENTLY, at their request, I met with two Special Investigators from my state's Department of Revenue at my favorite sandwich shop, *Amato's.* They announced to me that their purpose for the meeting was to investigate me for possible criminal and civil violations of my state's Revenue Code. Several years ago, and repeatedly, I had asked the state to inform me what "Dollar" meant on the tax forms, for my little hand-woven rug craft, but I never got a comprehensible reply. So I looked up Federal statutes for a definition of "Dollar." No one had ever paid me in gold or silver, so I assumed I have had no Dollar income and owed no Dollars.

One the agents advised me of my right to remain silent and to have an attorney present. Then asked me my full name. I chose to remain silent (*my name is my private property and I don't have to give it away*) and all other questions that would make their investigation into my finances a piece of cake.

Uniquely in America, we are under no obligation to provide **private information** that can be used against ourselves. Further, the fact that we choose not to give information, cannot be used against us, either. **Silence does NOT presume guilt.** Yet, how many Americans know this? Aside from Article 1 Section 10, the 5th Amendment is the main reason I intend to forever remain an American. It is the most wonderful guarantee of freedom from a potentially malignant government, in the whole wide world.

I got the distinct feeling that the agents respected my using my constitutional right against inquisition. They had heard my views on money before, back when they were investigating a friend of mind who had asked me along as a witness, and so that night they started posing questions about money. Not my money (*I wouldn't answer those questions*), but about money in general. They had been thinking about it, and wanted to know more. All three of us relaxed. Then I told them about Washington's letters during and after **the great Continental Inflation.** They hadn't known about that crisis. They hadn't known about Judge Roger Sherman's reasons for Article 1 Section 10, either. I told them about all my unanswered (*or evasively answered*) correspondence with state people begging them for a definition of "Dollar" used on their state forms. I told them that as soon as an officer of the state showed me where I was wrong, if I was wrong I would mend my ways at once. I also told them that they too, as much as you and I, have the power to save our personal finances from exploding in our faces.

"But if we went to a redeemable currency," one of them said, "what would happen to the balance of payments, interest rates, the IMF, international trade, things like that?"

"If we had gold and silver money again," the other said, "wouldn't the banks go broke? Wouldn't all government collapse?"

That's "the debate trap", I told them. Experts can filibuster day after day, week after week, month after month, year after year. **"What if" is the most potent**

weapon the Friends of Paper Money have. Debate and indecision merely fertilize inflation.

The best illustration I could think of was believing in God. If you sit down and try to figure out the consequences of living by God's program, you'll be so busy projecting, calculating, figuring, you'll never get around to committing to Him. The way to believe in God, as any minister will tell you, is to assume He is Truth and just begin operating by His system, no questions asked; like an automatic pilot. If Truth is good, then good things will happen to you. If Truth is good, should bad things threaten you, you'll know innately how to ward them off.

Clinging to Truth, that's all. It's the simplest thing in the world. *Clinging to Truth automatically summons good consequences.* Right things just fall into line. Debates and indecision evaporate. You're free just to be happy. That's what God (who is all Good) is all about. I've never known a person to choose God and be dissatisfied with his choice, have you? On the other hand, I've known many people who postpone and debate, postpone and debate, trying with their masters-degree-intellects to reason and predict outcomes. For their trouble, they seem always plagued with some inexplicable disorder. Some malfunction that needs attention. Their problem is that they try to evaluate in each and every situation, which would be the more profitable act: the truthful or the *un*truthful. They are the prisoners and practitioners of "Situation Ethics," and they're so busy with their constant debate they haven't time to relax and enjoy the great beauty of life.

The United States Constitution is so harmonious

with the simplest unchangeable laws of nature that I wholeheartedly agree with those who consider it to be in ways Divinely inspired. No other constitution of any other country in the world guarantees its people a government sworn to protect and defend individual freedom, freedom to be right, freedom to be wrong, and most importantly the freedom not to be tricked out of our property by some cleverly devised scheme — a clever scheme like paper currency promising redemption for gold and silver one day, then suddenly reneging on the promise after our precious metal has been taken away from us, as happened back in 1933. Whether it's one week or twenty years before you feel the effects of such a dirty trick, we have the freedom to blow the scheme's cover whenever we've had enough.

And it's guaranteed right there in Article 1 Section 10, in those **17 words** of Judge Sherman. Everyone else in the world is being systematically robbed of their property because they don't have a law against paper money. We have one but we don't know it. We know batting averages and the biographies of movie stars and pop-idols, but we don't know we have a law against economic tragedy, a law every public official from Main Street to Pennsylvania Avenue is sworn to support.

So, I told my friends from the Revenue Department, you don't need to be overly informed on interest rates, international payments, bond issues, gold prices, silver futures, or other consequences; and you certainly don't have to debate the pros and cons of obeying the United States Constitution. The choice is as simple as clinging to Truth or to Untruth. God and justice; or confusion and perjury.

Just OBEY that God-inspired United States Constitution, forget about the rest of the world (*is the rest of the world worrying about you?*) and good things will happen to you beginning right now. And in a way so vast and unexpected that it would be impossible to calculate in advance, even at M.I.T. Of course, some of the closer friends of paper money might have to revise priorities, just a little bit, but why shouldn't they? Shouldn't they pay a few dues after all they have over-charged us in the past?

The conversation lasted almost two hours then reached a warm and friendly conclusion. As we were getting up to leave, one of them said, "That part about not having to be overly informed, just believing in God and everything else falling into line, that makes a great deal of sense to me."

. . . The next evening, several good old boys who had been watching the interview apprehensively from across the room asked me if I'd been scared. "How can I be scared," I said, "when all I've done is obey the law those guys are sworn to uphold?"

"I deny the power of the general government to making paper money, or anything else a legal tender."

"The public welfare demands that constitutional cases must be decided according to the terms of our Constitution itself, and not according to judges' views of fairness, reasonableness, or justice. I have no fear of constitutional amendments properly adopted, but I do fear the rewriting of the Constitution by judges under the guise of interpretation."
— *Judge Hugo Black,*
in Columbia University's
Charpentier lectures, 1968

"The people can discern right, and will make their way to a knowledge of right . . . The appeal from the unjust legislation of today must be made quietly, earnestly, perseveringly; in a popular government injustice is neither to be established by force, nor to be resisted by force: in a word, the Union, which was constituted by consent, must be preserved by love."

12
Everyday Conversation

NOW that you understand the difference between paper and lawful money, and between law and hearsay, you're in a position to discuss things with persons in government. Educate them. Most of them have never had anyone bring up the constitutionality of paper money before. Don't harangue them or be rude. Honor your fellow man. Remember, they've done nothing wrong as long as people are willing to give them paper without objecting to its lawlessness. Here are some little things you can do.

TALK IT UP

Letters to various state and local officials in your town or county — and to your state representatives. Asking them if they enforce payment of taxes, fines, and other debts in anything other than gold and silver coin will alert them to the issue. And while you're at it, send a copy to your governor. Send your state's Attorney General a letter asking him for an opinion (*he's obliged to respond*): **"Is Article 1 Section 10 of the United States Constitution still binding on this state?"** *Get them all reading and talking.*

The subject is so touchy to many officials that they will probably answer you evasively, cunningly. In person, they may even make remarks and innuendos suggesting that you are nuts, but don't let this bother you. You are *right,* and they know it, rather they *fear* it. They're afraid that if you win, the *whole universe* will cave in on their heads. They have this fear because they've been educated (*as you and I*) by the Friends of Paper Money to think the problem is "very delicate"; "sensitive"; "complicated"; and completely out of their hands. **The idea-sphere says the problem is solvable only by the celebrities in Washington.** For many decades, our state and local officials have been conditioned to feel inferior: they're not as famous, not as well-paid, not as internationally glamorous as the Washington dignitaries. This creates a helpless attitude.

It's up to you to show your main street public servants that they have *incredible power.* Show them how the Constitution was written to give THEM ALONE the power to calm America's wild economic thrashings. THEM ALONE! Only THEY can kill financial confusion dead in its tracks by restoring the solid foundation of gold and silver coin. Tell them about Article 1 Section 10 and about *the money of account* of the United States.

Mention to the check-out girls and other clerks you encounter in a typical day that the tax they're collecting from you is *in unlawful money* and that you're not kidding. They're unknowingly conspiring with the state to violate the Constitution; tell them good-naturedly. Tell them that the reason food prices are soaring is that *increased paper amounts, increase prices* and that only the state can stop paper by refusing to make it legal tender. Tell them that they and the state are illegally making something other than gold and silver coin a tender in payment of debt. **The Constitution forbids enforcement of taxes by any state or local official in paper, plastic, copper, checks, or bank**

digits. And you don't have any gold or silver, because the Federal Reserve won't give you any. Tell them to ask old-timers if food prices don't remain relatively stable when paper is redeemable for gold and silver coin. Show them Article 1 Section 10. You could offer someone $1,000 to show you where that Article has been amended. You could even offer $10,000 to anyone who can show you a law that permits the state to circumvent Article 1 Section 10. You're 100% safe on both offers, as of 2003. You could offer a *million* and no one would be able to collect.

Let's discuss it with our minister, rabbi, or priest. The Constitution is the closest thing to Scripture there is. If it's the codification of the word of God in legal terms, it's certainly worth recommending from the pulpit and in counselling sessions and in Sunday School. Worth studying daily.

AVOID CONGRESSMEN AND SENATORS

Don't bother your Congressman about a redeemable currency. He's probably the greatest Friend of Paper Money in the country today. If you really want to hear some uneasy, extremely cunning word-speak, talk to your Congressman about reactivating our existing gold and silver monetary system. I don't recommend it unless he happens to be willing — *as a state citizen* — to impose Article 1 Section 10 upon high officers in state government. If not, he has the perfect excuse for copping out.

The Constitution empowers Congress "to borrow money on the credit of the United States," in borrowing from the Federal Reserve System, your Congressman and Senators are *merely carrying out their Constitutional mandate.* Your representatives in Washington are sweethearts of the Federal Reserve. The Friends of Paper Money contribute *gobs* to *all* the candidates and *lavishly* entertain the winners once in office. That's why you rarely if ever hear a peep of criticism of the American banking system out of Washington. If anyone is criticized it's *you,* for *"wasting"* our natural resources and oil, for buying too many things, for enjoying life, etc.

What Congress *can* do is try to balance the budget, which amounts to little more than scolding imaginary villains in the idea-sphere. And while Congress can't object to paper tender, it enacts legislation permitting the reduction of standards of quality; in foodstuffs, investments, manufactured goods, and personal freedom — legislation requiring you to *lower* you standard of living in the name of "conservation" — for the express purpose of *enabling the value of your money to be further diminished.* Since your Washington representatives enjoy virtual immunity from inflation through cost-of-living raises they vote for themselves, they simply don't feel the chaos and pain in the same way you and I do.

No: as famous, as majestic, as well-groomed, as omnipotent, as *black-limousine-dignified* as Congress might seem to be in our minds, they are *absolutely helpless to initiate the action that will turn away the gathering storm.* Don't waste your time with Washington on this issue.

AVOID VOTING

We Americans treasure our most prized possession: our vote. There's something slightly unpatriotic about someone who doesn't use his vote to determine the course of his republic — or so we are told. The media are filled with urgings to vote. But what good is your vote if everyone up for election is ignoring the law?

When officials abide by the United States Constitution, the vote is our way of selecting the best persons and the best government. But if our officials are disregarding the Constitution, or allowing it to be broken without lifting a finger, *your vote is their licence to steal.* You are aiding and abetting a criminal activity. You are giving them your permission to take your property and control your life. If you give them that permission, many will take you up on it, because lots of folks *enjoy* controlling others and appropriating their property. If you vote for anyone that allows Article 1 Section 10 to be ignored, don't you deserve to be ravaged by inflation?

The vote is only a minor part of your influence over your public servants and it only works when the Constitution's money system is in operation. You might as well stay home on election day as long as the Constitution's money system is in mothballs, because you'll only be voting for violators or accomplices. (*Don't remove your name from the Registration Lists, however. You'd be giving up your right to serve on a jury, which is a thousand times more important than voting. On a jury, you become a judicial officer with as much if not more power as a judge!*).

LAWYERS

My personal experience is that many lawyers are

ignorant of the Constitution *as law.* They see the Constitution *as the point of departure* for Supreme Court "interpretations." To hear many lawyers tell it, the Constitution only means what the Supreme Court SAYS it means. This is pathetically not true. This is living in the legal idea-sphere. It's Supreme Court Worship at its best. Abraham Lincoln complained about Supreme Court Worship in his First Inaugural Address:

> *If the policy of the government upon vital questions affecting the whole people is to be fixed by decisions of the Supreme Court, then the people will have ceased to be their own rulers.*

The Supreme Court can't make laws. Only legisators can make laws. **The Constitution rules the Supreme Court, not the other way around.** The Supreme Court is simply *a court of last resort* that decides specific cases brought to it. It often refuses to hear cases. Too, it often refuses to judge cases. Imagine having waited years for a Supreme Court decision and then getting a statement like this made by Justice Brandeis in *Ashwander v. Tennessee Valley Authority, 297 US 288*:

> *A judge, conscious of the affability of human judgment, will shrink from exercising in any case where he can conscientiously and with due regard to duty and official oath decline the responsibility.*

Lawyers who depend too heavily on case law instead of the Constitution ought to be reminded that judges are sworn *to support the Constitution,* not case law.

I feel apologetic for having criticized lawyers. After all, I know a pretty good one who I'd like to think is a very good friend of mine. Let me call on a lawyer, then, to criticize lawyers. T. David Horton — a member of the bars of Nevada, Virginia, the District of Columbia, and the United States District Court for the 9th Circuit — said:

> The course that lawyers take called "Constitutional Law" frankly doesn't consist of studying the Constitution. It involves memorizing the catechism (studying the sophistries) by which one provision after another of our Constitution is construed out of existence. This is one reason why **in our present constitutional crisis** we find lawyers among those who are derelict, failing to advance any remedy to correct the situation.

Mr. Horton revealed the astonishing reason why lawyers are lacking in fundamentals of the United States Constitution. In the words of one young lawyer: *"There are no questions on the bar examination on the Constitution, so why should we bother with it?"*

The first step in **the restoration of America to happiness and economic prosperity,** will not, *cannot* occur in the voting booths, in the Superme Court, or among our lawyers, or anywhere at the federal level.

Our Constitution reserves the greatest amount of power not to dignitaries but to housewives and shop owners, workers, the people; just plain folks. The Miracle will happen right in your home town, right there on Main Street, and you and a few friends will start it there and pull it off. As Charles Reily said, "It will not be the lawyers, politicians, or bureaucrats who save America; it will be the people who work with their hands. Housewives, truckers, carpenters, factory workers,

and farmers will turn this country around."
And I would like to add *schoolteachers,* too.

You shouldn't shrink from being **your own lawyer.** *It's thrilling and it's fun, and more and more serious people are getting into it. Neophyte Constitutionalists can learn to be astute, well prepared amateur attorneys who use the courts' own rules to achieve victories for their families and themselves.*

"Teenagers are more frequent crime victims than adults are now or were during their youthful years. Two of every five high school students are victims of violent crimes including robbery, assault, and murder."

"He who walks with wise men becomes wise."
— Proverbs 13:20

"You see, the more we are conditioned by education and just living in a society which teaches us to think along certain lines, the easier we are to fool. The magician encourages us to follow one logical path — the one we are accustomed to follow in a normal situation — while he, unknown to us, takes an entirely diferent one to accomplish his illusion. Thus, the hardest people to fool are children, who take little for granted. The easiest are scientists."

"While young people are gathering flowers and nose gays, Let them beware of the snake in the grass."

13
A Lesson They'll Never Forget

MANY of the ugly, ridiculous fixtures in public education that parents and teachers feel so helpless to repair came about through the printing of paper money. Remember, it is paper money that makes possible projects like school bussing. Constitutional money would stop the deterioration of our school systems in a snap.

In Tennessee and probably in your state, too, all public schoolteachers are required to take an oath to support the Constitution of their state and of the United States. In Tennessee, those teachers "who refuse to take the oath . . . shall be immediately dismissed from the service." (TCA 49-1304). I assume that the punishment for perjuring that oath would be as harsh as for refusing to take it, wouldn't you? Maybe even harsher. Both instances would certainly show a disregard for the Supreme Law of the Land, to the thinking of any reasonable person.

So if you're a Tennessee schoolteacher you're a duly sworn Officer of the Constitution. *You are prohibited from making anything but gold and silver coin a tender in the payment of debts.* If you choose to take a paycheck of ever-depreciating paper when the law entitles you — *requires you* — to take gold and silver coin, what kind of model are you for young sensibilities?

Would you want *your* child to come under the daily

influence of a person who couldn't tell the difference between a solid gold disc and a paper rectangle?

Even if you're *not* a sworn Officer of the Constitution of you state, you can have enormous effect. Rather than engage in abrasive strikes for *higher* pay, for example, you can simply hold out for *lawful* pay. (*All people who receive paper money from cities, counties, or states could do this*). That way, you'll be getting *both* higher and lawful pay. Pay that will hold its value year after year. Your pension will be worth something when you retire.

All that paperwork that's driving you nuts; it would stop expanding over night with the reactivation of gold and silver coin, soon slowing to a trickle all other dumb projects. And you'll be free to settle down to what attracted you to school teaching in the first place: *helping youngsters learn how to succeed in life.* Isn't that the true joy of teaching?

You could teach

THE LESSON OF THE TUMBLE-BUGS

the untold story of the earliest money manipulation.

Scarabs are little stones carved in the shape of beetles. The carvings were introduced into Egypt in 2200 B.C. after a great natural catastrophe destroyed much of the land. The Hyksos (*"Shepherd Kings"*) brought the idea from Mesopotamia, the birthplace of central banking, writing, military conscription, world war, and juryless trials. It took less than five minutes for a carver to make a scarab, whereas its equivalent in gold took many hours to mine and refine. The live beetle — we call them *Tumble-bugs* in Tennessee —

rolls amorphous animal waste into perfect spheres, like reconstucting a destroyed planet into a brand new one. Tumble-bugs bury the spheres of waste in the ground, enriching the soil. Because of their good work, and because their stone likeness, uplifting mottoes, and names of officials (*like all artificial "bank" money*), the native Egyptians trusted in them. They freely, enthusiastically, traded their gold and silver for them.

Gradually, the Hyksos officials pulled the gold and silver off for themselves, leaving an ever-increasing supply of scarabs to circulate. Dream money. The scarabs became worth whatever the Hyksos said they were worth. Since officials determined the value of human labor, they could direct human beings to dumb projects like building the pyramids!

The pyramids (*there are about 36 major ones in Egypt*) may be beautiful and very scientific, but they are really dumb. With a country's manpower building pyramids — or fighting wars or making costly things that get lost in outer space like today — agriculture operates at a bare minimum. Ask any farmer what he gets for his precious produce. This means scarce food. Scarce food means that food must be controlled by a central bureau. The Hyksos used the Egyptians' own gold to buy grain from other nations. To eat the Egyptians had to go, scarabs hand in hand, to the central storehouses, hoping that the officials were in a good mood.

So you see, controlling populations by lifting their money into the idea-sphere is old hat. The same rules apply today. They apply for all time. There will always be attempts to hook people on artificial money.

Of all the lessons alert teachers could give on

money, the most exciting one would be the LESSON OF LIVING BY THE CONSTITUTION. It would be an object lesson.

In Tennessee and in many other states it is a teacher's duty, required by law, "To teach the Constitution of the United States and of the state . . for the purpose of instructing all the children as to their privileges and duties under the said constitutions and for the promotion of good citizenship." (TCA 49-1307).

What a wonderful opportunity for your pupils to witness history in the making! You, their teacher, exercising your Constitutional Oath, demonstrating every American's economic rights, privileges, and duties in demanding that your paycheck be redeemable in gold and silver coin (*Article 1 Section 10*) at a value regulated by Congress (*Article 1 Section 8*)!

Your pupils would be seeing the power of the people flexing right there in the classroom and being felt and responded to under the Capital Rotunda in Washington. Much of the material sent you from Washington is subtly designed to belittle you and your students, which is one of the reasons people are so edgy and volatile. But the Supreme Law of the Land specifically provides that if *anyone* is to belittle *anyone,* it's to be the *other way around. You* belittle *Washington*! As you steadfastly abide by your Constitutional Oath, your pupils will be experiencing firsthand how their teacher — a state officer, armed with Roger Sherman's **17 words** — can require Congress to take steps to restore a lawful economy to this country.

It will be a lesson by which all lessons will be judged.

It will be a lesson they will never forget.

"Wisdom gives strength to the wise man more than rulers that are in a city." — Ecclesiastes 7:19

"In America a new people had risen up without king, or princes, or nobles, knowing nothing of tithes and little of landlords, the plough being for the most part in the hands of free holders of the soil. They were more sincerely religious, better educated, of serener minds, and of purer morals than the men of any former republic. By calm meditation and friendly councils they had prepared a constitution which, in the union of freedom with strength and order, excelled every known one before; and which secured itself against violence and revolution by providing a peaceful method for every needed reform. In the happy morning of their existence, as one of the powers of the world, they had chosen justice for their guide."

14

Miracle On A Maine Street, U.S.A.

THE MIRACLE began in the early months of the new millennium, on a Maine Street in the U.S.A.

One afternoon, a housewife, whose husband is a lawyer, called me at home to narrate her story. She was almost breathless with jubilance.

"I stayed up all last night to read your book. This morning my daughter and I drove to our local department store and bought $52.00 worth of merchandise. I told the cashier that this would be an **Article 1 Section 10 no-tax purchase.** She'd never heard of one of these, so she asked the manager.

The housewife explained to the manager that his company is a corporation, a creature of the state, therefore bound by any Constitutional prohibitions against a state. Since no state could make "any thing" but gold and silver coin a tender in payment of debts, his store was powerless to make anyone pay a state tax in "any thing" other than gold and silver coin. It being impossible to buy such coin in face amount equal to the sales tax, she chose not to "voluntarily pay" the tax in base-metal coin or paper money not backed by silver or gold.

Perplexed, the manager called the state department of revenue, and they told him — what else? — to collect the tax.

"I stood my ground and said that I was buying the goods, but not paying the tax," the housewife told me. "I counted out $52.00 and gave them to the cashier, took the merchandise, and headed for the front door. "This stuff is paid for, I told the manager. If you don't like it, do what you have to do."

Revelling in the Constitution's economic power, she and her daughter drove away in their yellow Corvette.

"About six blocks down the road," she said, " we were overtaken by several police cars. They made us get out of our car. They referred to us as "shoplifters" and such, and escorted us down to the police station. I was scared. At the station, the city attorney was there, and several other officers, and a man from the department of revenue.

"I cited a page of your book," she continued, "and said 'can't you see? **You're prohibited from taxing anybody in anything but gold and silver**?' These men raised their hands, and said, "Don't tell us that; we don't want to know that!'

"It was like waving garlic and a silver cross at a vampire," she exclaimed.

"Before long, the city attorney got up and said, 'Well, I'm leaving,' and then the tax man got up and left, and the booking officer closed the statute book he was thumbing through. 'Lady,' he said, 'I can't find that you've broken the law, so I guess I'll have to let you go.'

"And so we left.

"I'm going to talk to my husband, who is a lawyer, about suing them for false arrest, but I don't want to do that, I just want you to know that this is the most exciting thing that's ever happened to me in my life!"

And that was just a beginning on that day.

A certain municipal judge was so impressed with **the Constitutional solution** to our economic woes that he began reading "money rights" to anyone facing a fine in his court. His "money rights" warning was praised by all lovers of the Constitution:

> *It is clear by Article 1 section 10 of the United States Constitution and by Title 31 section 371 of the United States Code that this Court can only make gold and silver coin a tender in payment of debts. However, this Court will accept other forms of money such as Federal Reserve notes or personal checks if **voluntarily** tendered.*

Another report concerns a man who had been driving with an expired license plate. His defense was that he was driving with precisely the license plate the state required of him to have, since (a) the state had no authority to compel him to pay for the plates in paper money, and (b) he couldn't purchase the plate because he could not redeem Federal Reserve notes in their face-value equivalent in gold and silver coin.

The judge understood his position and reached a Constitutional compromise:

> *The Court finds you guilty because you still don't have a registration but I will not impose a fine, because I don't want you to pay the Court in gold or silver if you do not have it.*

Many enlightened Miracle-Workers have written letters to their state attorney general asking if Article 1 Section 10 is still binding on the state. Many attorney-generals suggested that the petitioner consult with a private attorney.

One western-state Miracle-Worker sought the advice of his county's official prosecuting attorney — and had been doing so for more than 10 years! His state's attorney general finally wrote:

> My opinion to your inquiry regarding the payment of your tax debt . . . is applicable to any state . . . **Article 1 Section 10 requires the state . . . to denominate your tax debt in gold and silver coin.** Unless and until the state authority denominates your tax in gold and silver coin, you are legally immune from such a tax, since any assessment repugnant to Article 1 Section 10 is absolutely void . . . The stereotyped response by the state attorney general is to cite the federal legal tender law and peremptorily claim that it overrides the state's obligation under Art. 1 Sec. 10. That this mandate of Article 1, Section 10 comes from the U.S. Constitution itself and is the supreme law of the land. The feds can ensure their fiat paper money decree for payment of debts between individuals and for payment of federal taxes and debts, but not between states and their citizens.

Pure economic justice is marvelously working its course: Just as the Friends of Paper Money withdrew gold and silver from circulation, the people on our Main Street are withdrawing from their obligation to pay debts in a form of money prohibited by law.

But that's just the half of it. They're also demanding that states deliver the dollars specified on their bank drafts! A Missouri dentist received checks totalling $668.20 as compensation for dental services. He demanded payment in silver coin, and was refused. He forthwith sued for a declaratory judgment against the state, and the court denied the state's motion to dismiss. Ordered by the court to explain why it couldn't pay out silver, the state's excuse was (*in a nutshell*) "We don't have any."

Literally thousands of awakened American are bringing to a grand and happy crisis this crazy economy we live in. How will it resolve? With an almost laughable simplicity. If you think that restoring silver and gold to our monetary system will require a difficult and tortuous journey through the corridors of Congress, read the United States attorney General's opinion, attached to 31 USC 311 in the federal statutes:

UNLIMITED COINAGE OF SILVER
The President has authority to proclaim and put into effect a plan for the unlimited coinage . . . of domestic silver produced after the affective date of the proclamation.
— *1933, 37 Op. Atty. Gen. 344, 1t 31 USC 311.*

And so, appropriate state authorities will inform the President that their state is having trouble with its commercial and public revenues because the people are standing on the Constitutional prohibition against irredeemable paper. (*I'll give a prize to the first state to reach the White House with this complaint. Keep us posted of your advances, by all means*).

With the utterance of a few words and the flourish of a pen, our money will be locked into a permanent value. *Inflation will literally be scribbled away with the signing of a man's name.* I suspect, in fact, that the Proclamation is already written and that new redeemable paper notes have already been prepared and are simply waiting for you to call them out.

You must understand, though, that it is not your

responsibility to petition the President for redeemability. **It is your state's responsibility.** You've got better thing to do with your time and energy. The state is your *servant,* remember. Let your *servant* do the work. Redeemability will be restored in the way redeemability has always been restored. It's a very routine operation, and the Friends of Paper Money know it by heart. They've been doing it for centuries.

The new paper will buy *United States Treasury* money, and it will be redeemable dollar for dollar in gold and silver coin. Irredeemable Federal Reserve paper, too, if the Fed people can escape the restoration with their reputations intact. It will promise redemption just like United States Treasury money. It will be a very smooth transition with no hard feelings if it happens before tragedy strikes.

If the Miracle were to happen as I write this, one United States Note would be worth one dollar of silver or 13 Federal reserve paper dollars. The new pricing would be denominated in both new United States Notes and old Federal Reserve paper. Since paper and silver and gold would be exchangeable again, there would be no need to hoard precious metals, and we would once again be able to experience that delicious sound of silver coins ringing on counter-tops. Our beautiful real money would creep out of hiding.

A gallon a gas would cost $1.30 Federal Reserve paper, or one silver dime. Imaging gasoline at 10 cents a gallon! A can of tuna fish, about a dime, too. A great suit of clothes $20 United States notes, or $260 Federal Reserve paper.

Stable prices, year after year!

The American Dream would be over before it

lapses into madness. The monetary system that allows dreamers to snap their fingers and have funds for whatever they can scheme up without any concern for whether there is demand or need for it would be gone. The monetary system that creates War and subsidizes drug addiction and all its crime and family-shattering and heartbreak would be gone. The monetary system that drives truckers and pricing boys and small businessmen and elderly pensioners and struggling young couples crazy, the monetary system that makes rich men out of debtors and poor men out of savers, that rewards incompetency with unexplained projects, that makes perversity the fashion, that celebrates the flames of violence, that favors untruth over truth, this system would be forever gone. The Friends of Paper Money would be free to invest solid money in worthwhile projects people really want.

And, miraculously, no one would be hurt. Value would return. There would not only be jobs galore, but jobs doing things for which there is real demand. Genuine pride of workmanship would be naturally restored. A person's value would again be determined by his good deeds, not by his inside connections or his knack for finagling and covering up.

Because a sense of the value of one's property would be restored, a sense of privacy, too, would return. With a healthy sense of privacy comes a natural revulsion for pornography. An esteem for one's own property and privacy naturally turns one's attentions away from celebrities in whose lives we are invited to live vicariously. Who needs to live a celebrity's life or in a soap opera's plot when his own life has value, esteem, interest, and excitement?

Gold and silver coin, being rare, precious, and easily accounted-for, automatically guarantees wise and prudent government spending. Violators are easily detected, dishonored and removed from office. (*Because it is impossible to account for artificial money, corruption flourishes in a paper economy*).

With gold and silver money, the United States budget would balance itself.

The people would express needs to one another and fulfill them among themselves, without government assistance. Costly projects no one wants (*no one, that is, except the lobbyist*) would shrivel and blow away for lack of demand.

Hands once considered untalented would begin turning out marvelous products. A joyous return to . . . *quality!*

Our children would grow up knowing they have genuine value. Because we rejected money that said "I don't now what I'm worth," we would stop hearing our teenagers say "I don't know what I want to do." The "use me" aimlessness of adolescence would vanish and leave solid purpose. Cheating would become deplorable again, instead of quasi-honorable as it is in many circles today. The love between boy and girl would cease to be a make-out project and would become instead a sensitive comparison of real values. Marriages would be built *not* on dreams but on facts and abilities. Conversation would make sense. Life would become *too thrilling* for the distractions of dope.

There would no longer be a need to seek escape, since being here would be so real and delightful and rewarding.

Our lives would be so worth living that suicide would be reduced as an option among the cures of our ills. Suicide and paper money march hand in hand, side by side throughout history. Since the most important plank of the Communist Manifesto is control of a county's wealth through the issuance of paper money from a central bank, our restoration of Constitutional money will eliminate communism and socialism as menaces to our freedom. Communism and socialism wouldn't make interesting topics in news, in classrooms, or debates.

Perhaps the greatest relief would be felt by those public servants who today suffer from the nagging awareness that they are living a lie; at last, they'd be free of the terrible pressures of covering up their sins against the Constitution — the Supreme Law of the Land they have pledged their honor to support and uphold.

Yes, everyone will benefit from the Maine Street Miracle: bureaucrats, rich, poor — even the Friends of Paper Money. We know this because gold and silver money invariably benefits all resourceful people.

The Constitution is proof of that fact!

"God did not make death, and he does not delight in the death of the living; the generative forces of the world are wholesome and there is no destructive poison in them." — *The Wisdom of Solomon 1:13,14*

15
Understanding Government
for what it really is

CONTRARY to what TV, magazines, radio, and newspapers say, government is meant to occupy a very small part of our experience. (*We must always remember that the media are usually beholden to government, or at least they think they are*).

For all the millennia man has existed, he's only had government for a little less than 6,000 years. So government has occupied only a very small part of man's natural history. But in those little less than 6,000 years government has done considerable damage. It has done lots toward pruning our species.

A Norwegian statistician computes that in the 56 centuries man has fought 14,531 wars. This is 2.6 wars per year. More than 600,000,000 men, women, and children have been killed by government. (*I dread to compute how many people our own government has exterminated*).

In more than 880 generations, there have been no more than 10 meagre years of true peace. Think about it.

There is an old legal maxim "No man shall be without law." Government arises out of man's need for law. If man cannot govern himself, officials rush in to do it for him. There is always that constant pressure to have law, natural or otherwise. One of the great, life-serving purposes of government, I believe, is to test man's need for law. If man needs law — if he fails to show that he can take care of himself and his own — government overcomes him. This is consistent with the way things work in nature. If a rabbit shows that he cares so little for life that he relaxes his vigilance, the eagle moves in and takes it from him, quick as a wink.

Since government lives by virtue of helpless people, government invests in keeping people helpless. The best way to keep people helpless is to *tell them constantly how helpless they are.*

Show them much crime, much menace, much mental derangement, much accidental death, much violence, much **terrorism.** Frighten them. Demonstrate to them how the only resolution to their dilemma is government. Send them to lawyers and accountants who are sympathetic or beholden to government. Circulate the proverb "You can't beat City Hall." Oppress them, and then . . .

And then what? Where does it lead? Once government has finally oppressed and expropriated every last soul on this planet, a strange phenomenon will happen. Oppression is not natural. Animals in cages live only a fraction as long as they live in the wild. Pretty soon, that world government will be faced with the ugly problem of death as a way of life. The leaders of government will have made a menagerie of dead animals. Everywhere they look, nothing but death and near-death. The architects of tyranny will grow miserable with their monstrous handiwork.

And that proposition reveals a solid gold secret. For, you see, government — that bloody beast of 600,000,000 corpses — *loves* strong people able to govern themselves. Although spokesmen will never tell you so, government loves free people able to resist government. This is why so many of our laws have little loopholes in them that excuse free people, people with so healthy and overpowering a determination to be naturally independent of government that they automatically spot legal clauses that strike discord with the higher, simpler law of God.

Government admires the fitness of people who are able to govern themselves, just like Hemingway admired, *loved,* the Great Fish for escaping in the final moment of that brutal struggle in *"Islands In The Stream." ***But it is government's duty to *challenge* the individual, to test his mettle, to determine for certain his convictions and abilities. This is material selection.**

Government chains, cages, or consumes the ones who surrender under its fearful threats and examples, but is *most fond* of the few that legitimately get away. These are the memorable ones.

Government propaganda likes to refer to any motion contrary to the prevailing drift as "rebellion" or "revolution" or "strike." Fearful words, words that make you tremble. Who wants to get involved in a rebellion? Leave that kind of monkey business to the rabble rousers.

This little book doesn't advocate any kind of insurrection whatsoever. As I told you earlier, you can make a lifesaving miracle happen simply **by declining to break a law.** If that's rebellion, then things really ARE topsy-turvy.

Here, in summary form, is what you have read:
1. **Irredeemable paper money** is the only cause

of your family's growing financial distress.

2. **There is absolutely no cure** for irredeemable paper money except to make it redeemable in gold and silver coin.

3. **You have an undebatable,** specific, ironclad Constitutional right to enjoy a money of gold and silver coined and regulated in value by your representatives and senators in Congress.

4. **Absolutely no one** has the power to require Congress to provide us with this solid money system immediately except your state and local government officials. Only your state and local government officials — not Congressmen — are prohibited from making paper a tender in the payment of debts.

5. **Your state and local government officials** will not act until you *tell* them to. Most of them are completely unaware of their power over the United States Congress and the Federal Reserve Board. Remember, your state and local government officials suffer from propaganda fallout, too.

5. **The "Declaration of rights"** of most state Constitutions guarantees you the indefeasible and unalienable right to see that your local and state officials obey their Constitutional Oath. Certainly the U.S. Constitution does. Would this right not include withholding payment of any state, local or corporate debts in a tender prohibited by the U.S. Constitution? Or demanding that state and local government and corporate paychecks be denominated in redeemable currency?

7. **The law requires** all public offices and courts to keep and have their accounts and proceedings in dollars of **"The money of account of the United**

States." Federal Reserve paper money has never been declared to be **"The money of account of the United States"**: it functions as such only because we allow our officials to break the law. No court or administrative official has any lawful authority, whatsoever, to require you to pay in something other than **"The money of account of the United States."**

8. **Once redeemability is restored,** you and your family will immediately enjoy a "sense of prosperity and tranquillity that could hardly have been hoped for." You have George Washington's word on it.

9. **Redeemability will cause no sudden panics** or painful reversals of fortune for anybody, not even the Friends of Paper money. As I write this, Federal Reserve paper dollars are already **unofficially redeemable** (*at coin shops*) at about $13 to $16 per silver dollar, gold a little higher. With official redeemability, paper dollars would merely remain at this price, and would circulate alongside United States Notes, which would be redeemable dollar for dollar in silver and gold. Gradually, the Federal Reserve paper dollars would be phased out.

10. **You need to ask yourself seriously:** If you neglect to take advantage of your lawful, God-insured economic rights **by obeying the law** are you not neglecting God, and would you not deserve the curse of economic catastrophe?

"A new public opinion must be created privately and unobtrusively. The existing one is maintained by the press, by propaganda, by organization, and by financial influences which are at its disposal. The unnatural way of spreading ideas must be opposed by the natural one, which goes from man to man and relies solely on the truth of the thoughts, and the hearer's receptiveness for new truth."

"For America the gates of revolution are shut and barred and bolted down, never again to be thrown open; for it has found a legal and a peaceful way to introduce every amelioration. The Constitution is to the American people a possession for all ages."

EPILOGUE
The Status Quo Illusion

WHEN you finish reading a book recommending action, you ponder alternatives and say to yourself, "I can either do what the book suggests or maintain the status quo." Now, I personally like the status quo. I believe that the *status quo-situation,* as is — is the regime that produces the longest, happiest lives. Long live the status quo! EXCEPT. . .

Except that under paper money status quo is just an illusion. For under paper money, **radical change** is going on with each turn of the printing press, **social change over which you have no control.** Social change that costs you energy, having to work harder to make ends meet. Social change that makes you tense, wondering if you'll be next to loose your job. Social change that costs you happiness, complaining about how angry the latest moral dip — or dumb — project has made you. Social change that costs you health and tranquility, as a loved one slips out of control into booze or drugs or psychosis or crime or the draft — or early death.

Embracing the status quo in a society with a fluctuation, crisis-plagued paper economy is like dancing on quicksand.

Less than two years before the day of his funeral, President Kennedy signed into law under the pressure of the "Cuban Missile Crisis" a series of emergency measures. These measures stand today as

Executive Orders, waiting to be invoked by whichever President decides (*or whose advisors decide*) we are in perilous times. The surest cause of perilous times throughout the past 56 centuries has been inflation. If you choose to maintain the status quo in an ever-increasing tide of Federal Reserve paper, you are helping to create *the right moment* for these Executive Orders to be called into being. Signed on February 16 and February 27, 1962, **these documents give the President complete dictatorial control over your life.** He will exercise this control through a bureaucracy of unelected dignitaries and officials in the Office of Emergency Planning. **If they hurt you, you cannot vote them out of power; you have to submit to them.**

The bureau's control over your life becomes effective according to the language of the Executive Orders, "in any time of increased international tension *or economic or financial crisis.*"

Try to imagine yourself and your family living under these Executive Orders:

1. EXECUTIVE ORDER 10995 takes over all communications media.

2. EXECUTIVE ORDER 10997 takes over all electric power, petroleum, gas, fuel, and minerals.

3. EXECUTIVE ORDER 10998 takes over all food resources and farms.

4. EXECUTIVE ORDER 10999 takes over all means of transportation, and controls highways and seaports.

5. EXECUTIVE ORDER 11000 drafts all citizens into work forces under governmental supervision and

control.

6. EXECUTIVE ORDER 11001 takes over all health, welfare, and educational functions.

7. EXECUTIVE ORDER 11002 empowers the Postmaster General to register all citizens nationwide.

8. EXECUTIVE ORDER 11003 takes over all airports and aircraft.

9. EXECUTIVE ORDER 11004 takes over housing and finance authorities, designates areas to be abandoned as "unsafe," establishes new locations for populations, relocates communities, builds new housing with public facilities.

10. EXECUTIVE ORDER 11005 takes over all railroads, inland waterways, and public storage facilities.

11. EXECUTIVE ORDER 11051 designates responsibilities of the Office of Emergency Planning, gives authorization to put the above orders into effect in times of increased international tension *or economic or financial crisis.*

Under Richard Nixon, these Orders were combined into the single *Executive Order 11490,* which was polished up with a few minor amendments and signed by Jimmy Carter on July 20, 1979. And all it takes to push the button on this bonecrushing machinery is for the President to declare an *"economic or financial crisis."*

Is there a chance the *Maine Street Miracle* could start the crisis that pushes the button of totalitarian control? Of course not. No.

The Maine Street Miracle is a lawful act, or in Judge Sherman's words at the Constitutional Convention in

Philadelphia in 1787, *"a favorable crisis."* It is a self-correcting, *liberating* crisis. As you turn paper into gold and silver, the rising line on the crisis-graph suddenly veers down. You cause the prompt and orderly restoration of enterprise, credit, tranquility, and "prosperity that could hardly have been hoped for." **The Maine Street Miracle is the disappearing of the grounds for invoking the dictatorship of those executive Orders.** The Maine Street Miracle is a *good* crisis, like finding God. People would be so happy, any President shouting "Crisis! Crisis! Executive Order!" would be laughed at as a clown.

The Executive Order crisis is a different kind of crisis where the rising line of the crisis graph bursts totally off the graph. It bursts off the graph because the people don't object to paper money in the way that counts. If you won't bring the rising line of the crisis graph down to earth, it can only be assumed that you are delegating your authority to dignitaries. It doesn't matter whether you delegate your authority out of ignorance, or complacency, or an act of will. Your silence in a worsening situation is evidence of *a surrender of your lawful power.* It's your way of saying *"I'm without hope."* **You've handed the problem over to the officials and they deal with the problem by rewarding officials first.** The best part of their reward is getting to control your life. I have many friends who can already perceive this happening. Do you?

Why shouldn't a population blessed with the constitutional power to stop economic disaster, but which does not use that power, why shouldn't such a self-neglecting population be tyrannized, head to toe? Why shouldn't the rabbit dozing in the open field suffer the eagle's attack?

So you see? **Hanging on to the status quo in increasingly lawless times is actually the most violent kind of revolutionary behavior.** Not objecting to paper money is the most wild-eyed, trouble-making, rabble-rousing kind of social **terrorism.**

If your posture is "I just don't want any trouble," your only choice is to help perform the Maine Street Miracle. For trying to ignore the gathering storm, not wanting to discuss it, is an *active contribution* to lawlessness and your own destruction. You'd might as well be carrying a gun, shooting your friends, looting their homes.

Article 1 Section 2 of the Tennessee Constitution expresses it more adamantly than I have here:

Non-resistance against arbitrary power and oppression is absurd, slavish, and destructive of the good and happiness of mankind.

With these words **the law itself condemns you** as absurd, as slaveish, and as a destructor of happiness and good if you fail to resist the oppression and arbitrary valuation of lawless money.

What social action could be *more fun* than the *Miracle on Maine Street*? What social action could be more harmless and exciting than using *the law* to stimulate your state to force the President to call our precious coins out of hiding? (*Don't worry; it's still there, plenty of it*). The *Maine Street Miracle* is a hundred times safer than burning draft cards, or marching for decency, or burning crosses, or demonstrating for civil or equal rights, or demonstrating against bussing, or chasing Iraqean students out of town. It's safer because there's no demonstrating necessary. It's a personal thing. It's between you and the folks at City Hall, you and the folks behind the counters of the shops that open out on main street, you and your friends, you and me. It's done not with courageous, bold proclamations but **with polite inquiries** like, "What has this state declared to be legal tender in the payment of debts?" "Are you upholding your oath to support Article 1 Section 10?"

The *Maine Street Miracle* will be the only truly powerful social movement where courage and daring are *not* fundamental requirements. It will be performed not by rabble but by nice, God-respecting people, from school children to old timers. Especially old timers, who contributed silver coin to Social Security only to receive paper dividends that buy less and less with each passing day. If they put silver in, shouldn't they get silver out?

One thing you'll not have to do as you achieve the Maine Street Miracle *is fight.* I believe that the concept that "personal liberty is something that must be fought for" is an old, old figment of the idea-sphere concocted by artful official propagandists.

Do you remember the widely-circulated conservative slogan of the 1960's, "Better dead, than Red"? The actual effect of this supposedly patriotic sentiment was the exact opposite of its supposed intent. "Better dead, than Red" prompted the more reasonable listener to begin calculating how many of his freedoms he could surrender to Communist invaders and still remain relatively comfortable. The phrase might as well have been coined by Khruchev himself.

Official propagandists have always depicted freedom as something that must be *earned* through bloody ordeal. Look at such emblems of liberty as war movies, the wounded fife and drummers marching in Revolutionary America. What is the purpose of these emblems? To encourage us to follow their example. For all the reverence and thanksgiving and piety they might inspire, they fail to encourage me to do anything but seek an alternative to fighting or suffering or dying at the hands of a liberty-robber. I'm not a martyr, and I don't believe you are, either.

No, I believe images of bloody ordeal are carefully designed to challenge the public imagination with the demand — THIS IS THE PRICE OF LIBERTY; ARE YOU WILLING TO PAY IT?

And most people — the best people, those who really love their families and enjoy every instant of being alive and healthy — decide the price is just a bit too high. And so they give up some liberty, some integrity, a few of their private rights, in order to avoid a fight. **What they overlook is that in the United States of America, bloody ordeal is *not* the price of liberty.** The Constitution overruled the "Fight for Rights" when it was ratified in 1789. Our Constitution guarantees "against violence and revolution by providing *a peaceful method* for every needed reform," as George Bancroft wrote.

If our officials should act adversely to the Constitution, upsetting our tranquility, we simply **remind** them that they are wandering from the law they are sworn to follow. We **'remind'** in America, not fight. Reminding is easier, more humane than fighting. Reminding is educational, bringing adversaries together in *under-*

standing rather than in *ordeal.*

The outcome is clean, profitable for all concerned, and there are no hard feeling. There is no fight involved in the *Maine Street Miracle.* It's a social action for scaredy cats.

Now that you've read this little book, you probably know more than many economics experts about the lawfulness of American money. More even than many lawyers and judges and government officials and professors. You now have the power to make the Maine Street Miracle happen:

Now work it on *your* Main Street!

APPENDIX

1
Little Known Facts

WHY DOES a merchant or lending institutuion always check your credit before providing you with its service when you as the *Sovereign* are the only source of credit in the world today? To find out what you know or don't know. To find out if you know the score (*of the commercial game*) or not.

Promissory notes can be tendered by the *Sovereign* to discharge debts in accordance with the Uniform Commercial Code at Sections 1-103, 1-104, 1-210(4)(28)(30), 3-104(a)(b) and *Public Policy—House Joint Resolution 192 of June 5, 1933* — as full satisfaction of any debt owed to a *Debt Collector* in response to his *Bill,* with a true and correct copy of said *Bill* attached thereto.

A Promissory Note is the *Sovereign's* promise to pay the *Bill* upon its endorsement and presentment at the *Sovereign's* location specified thereon.

By endorsing the *Sovereign's* Promissory Note the *Debt Collector* tacitly agrees that there is full satisfaction of his claim and that the *Sovereign* is discharged from liability on the alleged account. The obligation is *suspended* per UCC §§ 30319(b), 3-311, and 306-3, according to Public Policy: HJR-192.

The *Sovereign* does not waive timeliness, but if the *Debt Collector* needs additional time he can request an extension of time in writing with good cause shown. The acceptability of such a request is conditioned upon the approval of the *Sovereign.*

In the event that the Promissory Note is not presented for payment within a reasonable period of time, say 10 to 15 days, and there has been no written request for an extension of time with good cause shown, the *Debt Collector* tacitly agrees that the he has no *bona fide and verifiable claim* to the alleged account. The *Debt Collector* also tacitly agrees that it is his duty to prevent the alleged account from damaging the *Sovereign* in any way. He confesses judgment should the *Sovereign* initiate a counterclaim against him for filing a claim against the Sovereign's bond — and against all the *Debt Collector's* principals, agents and assigns whose acts and/or omissions result in tort damages against the *Sovereign*.

Take Note:

(1) A promissory note is a negotiable instrument — meaning money — according to UCC 3-104.

(2) A debt is fully discharged upon tender of a promissory note; it matters not if the promissory note is accepted or rejected, according to UCC 3-603.

(3) Nobody has an obligation to pay a debt in Federal Reserve Notes; per House Joint Resolution 192 of June 5, 1933.

(4) The one with the gold pays the bills.

House Joint Resolution 192
HJR-192 replaced Common Law with Public Policy on June 5, 1933. This congressional Resolution suspended our ability to pay our debts allowing only for their discharge.
Commercial paper (*a check, a draft, a Federal*

Reserve Note, a promissory note, etc.) passes the liability of an unpaid debt on to the recipient by a voluntary commercial transaction. Under Public Policy an unpaid debt carries a public liability for its collection hence all debt is now Public debt.

HJR-192 makes all forms of currency to be legal tender (*approved money*) for the so-called "payment" of both public and private debts. No one can refuse to accept the discharge of a debt tendered in any specific form of currency, since our sovereign credit is our currency. Anyone who demands otherwise is in breach of Public Policy: public Insurance policy HJR-192.

Congress established Public Policy (HJR-192) in 1933 and it has to be enforced and is enforceable by law. You can voluntarily discharge your debts pursuant to HJR-192 and a *Debt Collector* must give you a receipt showing payment in full.

HJR-192 of 1933 in simplified form says:

> Be it Resolved that every provision which purports to give a debt collector a right to require payment in a particular kind of coin or currency is declared to be against public policy. Every obligation shall be discharged upon payment, dollar for dollar, in any currency which at the time of payment is legal tender for public and private debts. Coin or currency means coins or currency of the United States including Federal Reserve Notes, notes and circulating notes of Federal Reserve banks and national banking associations (*including your promissory notes*).

In 1933 Congress entered the United States into bankruptcy and suspended the payment of all debts in gold.

This terminated Common Law and instituted Public Policy. When a government goes bankrupt it looses its sovereignty — the United States lost its sovereignty in 1933.

On April 5, 1933, President Roosevelt issued an Executive Order *"forbidding the hoarding of gold coin, gold bullion and gold certificates"* and attached the penalty of a $10,000 fine or up to 10 years in prison. Hoarding was defined as holding more than $100 in gold. Two months later on June 5, 1933, the 73rd Congress, 1st session, passed HJR-192 — an Act "to suspend the gold standard and abrogate the gold clause."

Once again in other words:

> HJR-192 states that: Every provision which purports to give a debt collector a right to require payment in a particular kind of coin or currency is declared to be against public policy. Every obligation shall be discharged upon payment in any such coin or currency which at the time of payment is legal tender for public and private debts.

A *Debt Collector's* former Right to demand payment made only in Federal Reserve Notes is against Public Policy. Every obligation shall be discharged upon *voluntary request* and upon payment in any currency that is legal tender for public and private debt, such as a *voluntarily tendered* promissory note.

HJR-192 goes on to state, in effect, that the terms coin and currency can mean circulating promissory notes of national banking associations; and each individual who has activated a UCC Contract Account is a banking association or bank.

There is no real money in America today. Federal Reserve Notes are not United States Notes backed by gold and silver coin. Federal Reserve Notes are **Congress' I.O.U.s to the Federal Reserve Bank.** It is your federal government that is bankrupt — not you. You are the only source of "credit" that exists!

2

Tacit Procuration

"tacit," *adj.* 1. Implied but not actually expressed; implied by silence or silent acquiescence. 2. *Civil law.* Arising by operation of law; constructive. *Blacks Law Dictionary, 7th edition. p.1465.*

"procuration," 1. The act of appointing someone as an agent or attorney-in-fact. 2. The authority vested in a person so appointed; the function of an attorney. 3. PROCUREMENT. *Blacks Law Dictionary, 7th edition, p.1224.*

"procurement," *n.* 1. The act of getting or obtaining something . . . *Blacks Law Dictionary, 7th edition, p.1224.*

Tacit Procuration is a constructive act — arising by operation of law — of getting or achieving something by implied but not actually expressed silent consent resulting in contract agreement whereby a party has already testified to the truth of a matter and against himself.

A Tacit is constructive based on the act or the failure to act of the parties.

Tacit Procuration means that even though the party has not expressly answered a question or presumption at hand, it is presumed that he understands that his answer would be what the questioner or presumer assumes it to be.

In essence, the questioner or presumer is saying, "If you don't answer this question or presumption I will assume what your answer is intended to be. If you fail to respond, when you have a duty to respond, then by agreement of the parties as an operation of law, this has become your answer which you cannot change, because you had the opportunity to change it but did not."

For example: If the IRS sends you an invoice and you don't *object, protest,* or *accept it conditionally upon proof of claim,* your failure to respond is your *tacit agreement* that they have it right and this becomes your position. So a judgment (*self-confessed*) is already in before you even go to court. The judgment is your silent agreement obtained by Tacit Procuration.

THE PROCEDURE

1. A Claim is an offer to a Respondent, not a demand.
2. The Offeror is the tail and the Acceptor is the head.
3. An offer is a presentment of something for agreement or disagreement that commands a response.
4. There are three ways to respond to an offer:
   4.1. A respondent can accept the claim as stated;
   4.2. A respondent can present a counterclaim of a higher priority in truth;
   4.3. A respondent can stand mute.
5. When an offer is refused or ignored it is dishonored and the head becomes the tail and the tail becomes the head.

SILENCE IS ACCEPTANCE OF THE CLAIM.

3
Understanding Drafts

A DRAFT is an unconditional written order signed by one person (*the drawer, or maker*) directing another person (*the drawee*) to do some certain thing — to perform some certain act.

A check is the most common example of a draft. A check is an unconditional written order signed by one person (*the drawer*) directing another person (*the drawee or payer*) to pay a certain sum of money on demand or at a certain time to a third person (*the payee*) or to the bearer of the check.

Other examples of a draft are a Bill of Exchange, a Letter of Exchange, or a Note, or even a written or *verbal* communication.

"honor" means to "accept." To honor a draft is to accept it when presented and to honor it (*perform to it*) if it is honorable (*authentic*).

The question is: "Is it honorable or not?" "Is it an authentic draft or not?"

A draft is a written document that contains three things:

1. A certain order. (*specific written instructions; a certain sum*).

2. A date in time. (*the date it was made*).

3. An authentic signature of the maker. (*the person making the claim*).

A draft bestows on you a negative commercial energy that needs to be discharged by a positive action. Its maker is presenting a ball to you (*a "hot Potato"*) that you need to play (*get rid of*). If you "drop" the ball you default. And if you "hold" the ball you default. So throw the ball back to the maker and get HIM to default instead of you. If the maker drops the ball or holds the ball too long, he defaults and you win.

If you ask someone else to return your ball *for* you (*an attorney*) he might default in your stead. If so, he is in the clear but you bear the consequesces of his default. Therefore, handle the ball yourself, then no one else but you can make you default (*you stay in control*).

There are (5) ways to respond to a draft.

1. You can argue or explain. *You can attempt to persuade — and you default.*

2. You can demur. *You can object to legalities without admitting or denying*
the facts — and you default.

3. You can traverse. *You can deny the facts as allegations — and you default.*

4. You can remain silent. *You can hold the ball — and you default.*

5. You can accept the claim. You can **"agree with thine adversary quickly, whiles thou art in the way with him"**— *Matthew 5:25,* — and you just might win.

How can you "accept the claim" (*agree with the charge*) and still win?

If you unconditionally accept the claim, you hold the ball and you default. But if you accept claim subject to a condition that the maker can't meet (*proof of claim*) and "return (*the claim*) to sender", *he* ends up holding the ball and *you* win.

So, that's the name of the game. *Accept the claim on condition of proof of claim and return to sender.* A conditional acceptance is a counterclaim back to the sender that bestows negative commercial energy on him that he has to discharge — if he can — or he defaults.

Why does this procedure work? For two reasons:
1. The UNITED STATES is bankrupt.
2. There can be no controversy in bankruptcy.

Attorneys create controversy, to set you up to default; stay out of controversy to the bitter end and you win.

Remember:
1. A letter might be a draft; a letter *is* a draft if it contains an order or a demand.
2. A spoken order is *also a draft.*

If a judge orders you to "stand up" and you unconditionally stand up, you have just accepted his draft by your actions and confirmed a contract of agreement that you will deal with him; you've entered his arena, and you default.

It matters not who's right or wrong. All that matters is who holds or drops the ball, and who ends up *not* holding the ball in the end.

"It's the procedure, stupid." It's a "Hot Potato" game. Get rid of the "Hot Potato." Don't be holding the ball in the end.

Conditional acceptance is the honorable thing to do. If the conditions you stipulate are not met you win the commercial game.

"Blessed are the peacemakers for they shall inherit the earth."

MAINE STREET MIRACLE

"As we have therefore opportunity, let us do good unto all men, especially unto them who are of the household of faith." — Galatians 6:10.

Made in the USA
Coppell, TX
09 May 2024

32233576R00085